Upgrade
your Italian

Clelia Boscolo
UNIVERSITY OF BIRMINGHAM

Hodder Arnold

A MEMBER OF THE HODDER HEADLINE GROUP

A member of the
Hodder Headline Group
LONDON
Distributed in the United States
of America by Oxford University
Press Inc., New York

First published in Great Britain in 2005 by
Hodder Education, a member of the Hodder Headline Group,
338 Euston Road, London NW1 3BH

www.hoddereducation.co.uk

Distributed in the United States of America by
Oxford University Press Inc.,
198 Madison Avenue, New York, NY10016

Hodder Headline's policy is to use papers that are natural, renewable
and recyclable products and made from wood grown in sustainable forests.
The logging and manufacturing processes are expected to conform to
the environmental regulations of the country of origin.

The advice and information in this book are believed to be true and accurate
at the date of going to press, but neither the author nor the publisher can
accept any legal responsibility or liability for any errors or omissions.

British Library Cataloguing in Publication Data
A catalogue record for this book is available from the British Library

Library of Congress Cataloging-in-Publication Data
A catalog record for this book is available from the Library of Congress

ISBN-10: 0 340 80966 3
ISBN-13: 978 0 340 80966 2

1 2 3 4 5 6 7 8 9 10

Typeset in 10/12 pt Formata by Charon Tec Pvt. Ltd, Chennai, India
Printed and bound in Great Britain by CPI Bath.

What do you think about this book? Or any other Hodder
Education title? Please send your comments to the feedback
section on www.hoddereducation.co.uk.

Contents

Acknowledgements

First and foremost I would like to thank Dr Eva Martinez, Arnold's Commissioning Editor for Modern Languages, for her constant support and patience.

I am also indebted to my students in the Department of Italian Studies at the University of Birmingham, who have tried the material and have made many useful suggestions for its improvement; to my colleagues Mr Gerry Slowey and Miss Alessia Bianchi, who patiently read through each chapter and corrected many inaccuracies; to Dr Jonathon Dale and to my son, Edwin, for their time, patience and wizardry on the PC; last, but not least, to Stephen Harrison, without whose help, support and advice this book would be a much poorer effort. Needless to say, any remaining inaccuracies or omissions are entirely my responsibility. I would be grateful to receive comments on the book from colleagues and learners.

I dedicate this book to the memory of my father, Fiorello Boscolo detto Bragadin, and to my children Edwin and Maddalena.

Clelia Boscolo
e-mail: C.Boscolo@bham.ac.uk
August 2004

Introduction

Aims of the book

This book is aimed at students of Italian as a foreign language studying in a variety of learning contexts (preparing AS or A2 examinations, revising for their end-of-year examinations during degree courses, adult learners), who need to improve their written and oral performance. It is a 30-day revision and consolidation course designed to help learners overcome a series of basic grammatical errors, to improve and refine their topic-based vocabulary, and to add a degree of elegance and sophistication to their style, by working on their own with exercises that will take up to one and a half hours per day to complete.

It is not realistic to expect to master very complex and subtle aspects of the Italian language for the first time just before examinations and working on one's own. For this reason, this book does not aim to cover everything: a good reference grammar and a bilingual dictionary are invaluable learning tools, which should be used by all learners. *Upgrade your Italian* focuses on three key areas where a real difference can be made in a relatively short space of time:

- spotting mistakes and correcting/avoiding errors and oversights on key grammar points;
- making a conscious effort to use more accurate and adventurous vocabulary and idiomatic expressions;
- making a conscious effort to use a more sophisticated and elegant style and to be flexible in one's use of constructions.

In order to maintain interest and concentration, the chapters devoted to the three key areas alternate; and as consolidation of the previous days' work has been deliberately built into the programme, following the order of the book will allow maximum benefit from it.

Getting the most from the book

You should complete one chapter per day over 30 days. Material is absorbed and internalized better through steady, continuous work, rather than by cramming in several chapters on one day. If you want to do more language work each day, then do something other than *Upgrade*: go over vocabulary lists, revise some verbs, do some reading or some listening.

Some chapters will appear easier than others: alternating lighter and tougher material has been done deliberately, as it helps the learning process. Some words or expressions appear several times through the book in different contexts (sample phrases, exercises, vocabulary lists). This is also deliberate, as it helps to learn these expressions as separate entities.

Remember that material is truly absorbed only if it becomes part of your active language, i.e. you must be able to use it in your own work. So, include in your additional language work some writing or speaking activity in which to use the expressions you have learnt in recent chapters of *Upgrade*. The more you recycle and use the new material, the more quickly you will learn it.

You should spend no more than an hour and a half to complete each chapter. If you find you haven't finished in that time, leave it for at least a couple of hours and return to it later. Use a pencil: if an exercise is particularly tricky, you can rub your answers out and try again later on.

Check your work against the answer key at the back of the book and count your total of correct answers out of 30. If you have got fewer than 20 correct answers, you should do the chapter again, but not immediately. Leave it for an hour or two before going back and trying again. If your correct answers number between 20 and 29, rub out the incorrect answers and try doing them again the following day, before you start working on a new chapter. Make sure you understand where you went wrong before you proceed to the next chapter.

As well as doing the exercises and checking your answers, note down any new item of vocabulary or idiom and learn them. Always list nouns with their gender, and verbs with their irregularities and dependent prepositions. Make a conscious effort to improve your vocabulary learning strategies: find out what works best for you, i.e. what helps you learn more quickly and accurately. You can make lists of words and read them out loud or in your head, you can record and listen to them many times, put them on post-it notes around your room, write them down many times, or use them to make sentences. Learning new vocabulary is fundamental: it multiplies the possible expressions you can use, speeds up the learning process, and allows you to raise the register of your language.

Use the references to grammar books given at the end of chapters to look up any points on which you want or need fuller explanations: the explanations given in *Upgrade* do not aim to give exhaustive coverage, but instead focus on points which are known from experience to cause recurrent problems to learners.

Even more importantly, learn to correct your own work: by the time you have worked through *Upgrade* you will have a very good idea of where your major problems arise. Bear this in mind to work out your own checking strategy.

Applying what you have learnt

Depending on your individual needs, your checking strategy may include any or all of the following:

- the gender of nouns;
- the correct forms of the articles;

- adjectives/past participles for agreement;
- verbs for tense, formation and agreement with subject;
- pronouns (direct, indirect and relative);
- verb constructions and prepositions.

Methodical checking is a very good way to remedy many errors and slips of the pen which will make you lose marks unnecessarily.

As you write or check your work, be conscious of matters of vocabulary and style: look out for obvious Anglicisms and wrong spelling, try not to over-use the same basic words, aim for variety and accuracy. Be adventurous with your style and use of idiomatic expressions: they will help you gain some precious extra marks.

Most importantly, enjoy learning Italian! Buon lavoro e in bocca al lupo!

Key points: Agreement I – nouns and adjectives

DAY 1

Do you make mistakes with the agreement of adjectives and nouns? Learners expect the endings of nouns and adjectives in Italian to match every time, but they often don't. The following exercises will help you get your endings right.

I   Agreement for gender

Adjectives must agree in gender (masculine or feminine) with the noun they qualify. First, then, you must know the gender of the noun, checking if in doubt. Although most singular nouns ending in **-a** are feminine, some frequently used ones are masculine: **il cinema, il pigiama, il programma, il dramma, il poema, il problema, il tema, il clima, il sistema, il trauma, il dilemma**, as well as nouns referring to people like: **il collega, il poeta, il giornalista, il pediatra**.

Similarly, there are some nouns ending in **-o** which are feminine: **la mano, la radio, l'auto, la biro, la foto**.

Most Italian adjectives belong to one of three groups:

- adjectives ending in **-o**, which have the feminine singular form in **-a**, e.g. **italiano, italiana; necessario, necessaria; famoso, famosa;**
- adjectives ending in **-e**, which remain the same in the feminine, e.g. **inglese, interessante, facile;**
- adjectives ending in **-a**, which also remain the same in the feminine, e.g. **ottimista, entusiasta, egoista**.

Here are some sentences where the endings don't match:

Il cinema italiano ha sempre più successo.
[Italian cinema is ever more successful.]
Dov'è il mio pigiama verde?
[Where are my green pyjamas?]
Il clima inglese è davvero strano!
[The English climate is really strange!]
Ho una piccola radio portatile.
[I have a small portable radio.]
Chi non vorrebbe una Jaguar, la più prestigiosa auto inglese?
[Who would not want to have a Jaguar, the most prestigious English car?]

Now make the adjectives in the following sentences agree as necessary. The masculine singular form is given in brackets.

1-**3** **L'inquinamento (ambientale) è un problema (serio) e (difficile).**
Environmental pollution is a serious and difficult problem.

4-**5** **L'(ultimo) foto è davvero (bello).**
The last picture is really beautiful.

6-**7** **Mi presti la (tuo) biro (rosso)?**
Will you lend me your red biro?

Many singular nouns end in **-e**. Some are masculine and others feminine. Note the following patterns:

- Most nouns ending in **-ore**, **-ere**, **-ale**, **-ante** and **-ente** are masculine. (Notable exceptions are: **la capitale, la cattedrale, la corrente, la gente, la stampante, la mente**.)
- Most nouns ending in **-ione**, **-trice**, and **-ine** are feminine. (Notable exceptions are: **il fulmine, l'ordine, il pettine, il campione, il milione, il lampione**.)

These nouns can also be qualified by the types of adjective we have seen above. Here are some examples:

Questa torta ha un sapore molto delicato.
[This cake has a very delicate flavour.]
La tua non è una ragione valida.
[Yours is not a valid reason.]
Il libro offre un'immagine ottimista e cosmopolita del nostro quartiere.
[The book gives an optimistic and cosmopolitan picture of our area.]
Premendo questo piccolo pulsante rosso si ricarica la batteria.
[The battery is recharged by pressing this small red button.]

Make the adjectives in the following sentences agree as necessary. The masculine singular form is given in brackets.

8 **Prova ad usare un'espressione (diverso).**
Try and use a different expression.

9-**10** **Preferiremmo una soluzione più (realista): la questione è (complesso).**
We would prefer a more realistic solution: the matter is complex.

11 **L'infermiere (notturno) non è ancora arrivato.**
The night nurse has not arrived yet.

II Agreement for number

Adjectives must agree in number (singular/plural) as well as in gender with the noun they qualify. The plural of an adjective is formed according to the following pattern:

- Adjectives ending in **-o** will end in **-i** if masculine and in **-e** if feminine, so **italiani, italiane; necessari, necessarie; famosi, famose**.
- Adjectives ending in **-e** will end in **-i** both for masculine and for feminine, so **inglesi, interessanti, facili**.
- Adjectives ending in **-a** will end in **-i** if masculine and in **-e** if feminine, so **ottimisti, ottimiste; entusiasti, entusiaste; egoisti, egoiste**.

Here are the patterns for the plural of nouns:

- Nouns ending in **-o** will end in **-i**. Note that **l'uomo** changes to **gli uomini** and words like **auto, foto, moto, biro** and **radio** remain the same in the plural.
- Nouns ending in **-e** will also end in **-i**.
- Nouns ending in **-a** will end in **-e** if they are feminine and in **-i** if they are masculine. **Cinema** and **pigiama** remain the same.
- Nouns ending in a stressed vowel (**la città, il sofà, il caffè, il lunedì, la tivù**, etc.), foreign words (**il film, lo sport, l'autobus, l'Euro, la routine**, etc.) and the words **l'analisi** (f.), **la crisi, la diagnosi, l'ipotesi** (f.), **la metropoli, l'alibi** (m.), **il brindisi, la serie** and **la specie** remain the same in the plural.

As you can see, there can be several combinations of endings and in many cases the endings of nouns and adjectives won't match. Here are some examples:

In molte città italiane non c'è la metropolitana.
[In many Italian cities there is no underground.]
Non sempre le auto veloci sono pericolose.
[Fast cars are not always dangerous.]
Servono iniziative economiche efficaci, non soluzioni idealiste.
[We need effective economic initiatives, not idealistic solutions.]
Che domande difficili!
[What difficult questions!]

Now put the following combinations of noun + adjective in the plural:

12-**13**	**Il diritto fondamentale**	**I** ....
	The fundamental right	*The fundamental rights*
14-**15**	**La legge fascista**	**Le** ....
	The fascist law	*The fascist laws*

16-**17** La spiegazione insufficiente	Le ....
The insufficient explanation	*The insufficient explanations*
18-**19** La società occidentale	Le ....
The Western society	*The Western societies*
20-**21** La brutta abitudine	Le ....
The bad habit	*The bad habits*
22-**23** Il problema iniziale	I ....
The initial problem	*The initial problems*

It is fairly easy to remember to make adjectives agree when they are next to the noun they qualify, but be careful to make the agreement also when the adjective is connected to the noun by a verb like **essere, sembrare, diventare**. For example:

Le banche sono burocratiche, ma i centri commerciali sono efficienti.
[Banks are bureaucratic, but shopping centres are efficient.]
Le sue sorelle sono improvvisamente diventate grandi e belle.
[His/her sisters have suddenly grown up and become beautiful.]
La mamma di Piero sembrava gentile e generosa.
[Piero's mum seemed kind and generous.]

Be particularly careful in a relative clause; always check back to find the noun qualified by the adjective. For example:

Hanno trovato delle riviste che ci saranno veramente utili.
[They have found some magazines which will be very useful to us.]

Make the adjectives in the following sentences agree as necessary:

24-**25** Quelle ragazze non sembravano (capace) di essere così (violento).
Those girls did not seem capable of being so violent.

26-**27** Tutti quelli che erano (presente) alla riunione erano (entusiasta) della decisione.
All those who were present at the meeting were enthusiastic about the decision.

III Common problems with agreements

- If an adjective qualifies two or more nouns of different genders, e.g. **una stampante e un computer nuovi** [a new printer and computer], the adjective is masculine plural.

- Be careful to make the adjective agree with the noun it qualifies in phrases like:

dal punto di vista finanziario
[from the financial point of view] (masculine agreement with **punto**)
È uno dei quadri rinascimentali più famosi.
[it's one of the most famous Renaissance pictures] (the adjective describes all the pictures and so is plural)

- After **qualcosa, niente, qualche cosa**, use **di +** masculine adjective. For example:

qualcosa di buono
[something good]

- Past participles do not agree when they are part of a compound tense conjugated with **avere** (and there are no direct object pronouns). Otherwise they must agree with the noun or pronoun they refer to. For example:

Finalmente abbiamo finito di studiare.
[At last we have finished studying.] (no agreement because the past participle **finito** is with **avere**)
Finalmente la scuola è finita.
[At last school is finished.] (agreement because **finito** is with **essere**)

Make the adjectives in the following sentences agree as necessary:

> **28** Luisa soffre di mal di testa (continuo).
> *Luisa suffers from persistent headaches.*
>
> **29** Avete trovato qualcosa di (utile)?
> *Did you find something useful?*
>
> **30** Tutte queste lettere sono (scritto) a mano.
> *All these letters are written by hand.*

Now check whether your answers are correct. If you have scored 30 out of 30, you can consider this section finished. If you scored fewer than 20 out of 30, you should do it all over again, but not now. Do something else for at least an hour before coming back to it. If you scored between 20 and 29 out of 30, look back tomorrow at the mistakes you have made before starting the next section. Make sure you understand where and why you went wrong before moving on. Follow this procedure for each day you work on *Upgrade*.

See for further information
Soluzioni!, Chapters 1–3
A Reference Grammar of Modern Italian, Chapters 3 and 4

Upgrade your vocabulary: Describing people

DAY 2

A rich, varied and appropriate vocabulary is essential if you want to upgrade your Italian. These chapters aim to help you consolidate words and expressions you already know, to link them to others belonging to the same 'family', and to introduce new ones, on the same topic.

Learning groups of words that are related to each other is a very efficient way of building up one's vocabulary, which will make you a faster and more accurate reader and listener; it also helps you understand how the language is constructed, which will allow you to guess new words more confidently.

Here are eight groups of words relating to the physical description of people. Learn the ones you don't know by linking them in your mind to the ones you know already, then practise them in the exercises that follow.

gli occhi eyes
le occhiaie rings under one's eyes
le borse sotto gli occhi bags under one's eyes
un'occhiata a glance, a look
dare un'occhiata a to take a look at
l'occhiello buttonhole
costare un occhio della testa to cost an arm and a leg
fare l'occhiolino to wink

la faccia face
avere la faccia stanca to look tired
faccia a faccia face to face
sfacciato/-a cheeky
Che faccia tosta! What a cheek!

la bocca mouth
una boccata a puff (of smoke), a breath (of air)
prendere una boccata d'aria to go out for a breath of (fresh) air
sboccato/-a foul-mouthed
rimanere a bocca aperta to be taken aback (with astonishment)
rimanere a bocca asciutta to have nothing to eat, to be disappointed
In bocca al lupo! Good luck!

il viso face (higher register than **faccia**)
a viso aperto openly

la barba beard
la barbetta goatee
barbuto bearded
il barbiere barber
il barbone tramp
farsi la barba to shave
farsi crescere la barba
 to grow a beard

barboso/-a boring
Che barba! What a bore!

il naso nose
annusare to sniff
ficcare il naso negli affari altrui
 to poke one's nose into other
 people's business
ficcanaso nosy parker, busybody

i capelli hair
 sciolti loose
 legati tied
 rasati shaved
 a spazzola crew cut
 brizzolati grizzled
pettinarsi to comb one's hair
la pettinatura hairstyle

la carnagione complexion
 rosea rosy
 olivastra olive
 morbida soft
ammorbidire to soften
l'ammorbidente (m.) fabric
 softener

Sketch the appropriate features on the blank faces. To consolidate the rules on agreement covered in Day 1, add the missing endings:

1-**3** Marco ha i capelli cortissim _ , a spazzola, e una barbetta ner _.

4-**5** Mio padre ha deciso di farsi crescere la barba: adesso sembra un barbone un po' trist _.

6-**8** Che faccia stanc _ hai, mamma, e che occhiaie scur _! Non hai dormito?

Now complete the following sentences with the missing words:

9 Il film di ieri sera era orrendo, una vera _ _ _ _ _!
Last night's film was horrible, a real bore!

10 Il fratellino di Paola dice molte parolacce: è un bambino davvero _ _ _ _ _ _ _ _.
Paola's younger brother swears a lot: he's a really foul-mouthed child.

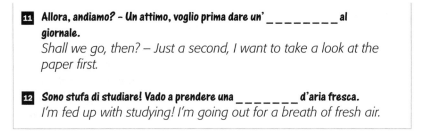

11 **Allora, andiamo? – Un attimo, voglio prima dare un'** _ _ _ _ _ _ _ _ **al giornale.**
Shall we go, then? – Just a second, I want to take a look at the paper first.

12 **Sono stufa di studiare! Vado a prendere una** _ _ _ _ _ _ _ _ **d'aria fresca.**
I'm fed up with studying! I'm going out for a breath of fresh air.

Here are ten groups of words relating to character. Again, use the ones you already know to help you learn the others.

l'umore (m.) mood
essere di buon/cattivo umore to be in a good/bad mood

l'educazione (f.) politeness, good manners
educato polite
maleducato rude

il carattere disposition, nature
avere un buon/brutto carattere to be good/bad natured

la pigrizia laziness
pigro lazy

l'orgoglio pride
orgoglioso proud

la testardaggine stubborness
testardo stubborn
essere testardo come un mulo to be as stubborn as a mule

l'avarizia meanness (with money)
avaro mean

la disinvoltura confidence
disinvolto confident

la comprensione understanding (n.)
comprensivo understanding, tolerant

l'inibizione inhibition
inibito inhibited
disinibito uninhibited

Now practise by doing this wordfit puzzle. Each time you fit a word into the grid, copy it against its meaning in the box which follows the grid. (Clue: start with the longest word first!) The shaded squares will give you the letters for one word that is missing from the grid. All nouns should appear in the grid with their definite article.

5 letters	6 letters	7 letters	8 letters	9 letters
avaro	l'umore	educato	testardo	l'avarizia
pigro		inibito		l'orgoglio

10 letters	11 letters	14 letters	15 letters
disinibito	il carattere	la comprensione	la testardaggine
disinvolto	comprensivo	la disinvoltura	
maleducato	l'educazione		
la pigrizia	l'inibizione		

13   *politeness*   _ _ _ _ _ _ _ _ _ _ _
     polite   _ _ _ _ _ _ _
     rude   _ _ _ _ _ _ _ _ _ _

14   *laziness*   _ _ _ _ _ _ _ _ _ _
     lazy   _ _ _ _ _

15   *stubborness*   _ _ _ _ _ _ _ _ _ _ _ _ _ _ _
     stubborn   _ _ _ _ _ _ _

16 *pride* _ _ _ _ _ _ _ _
proud _ _ _ _ _ _ _ _ _

17 *meanness* _ _ _ _ _ _ _ _ _
mean _ _ _ _ _

18 *inhibition* _ _ _ _ _ _ _ _ _ _
inhibited _ _ _ _ _ _ _
uninhibited _ _ _ _ _ _ _ _ _

19 *confidence* _ _ _ _ _ _ _ _ _ _ _ _
confident _ _ _ _ _ _ _ _ _

20 *understanding (n.)* _ _ _ _ _ _ _ _ _ _ _ _ _
understanding _ _ _ _ _ _ _ _ _ _ _

21 *mood* _ _ _ _ _ _
disposition _ _ _ _ _ _ _ _ _ _

The last group of words relates to clothing. When you have learnt the words, test yourself by doing the exercise that follows the list.

la camicia shirt
la camicetta blouse
la camicia da notte nightdress
il camice lab-coat, white coat
in maniche di camicia in shirtsleeves
sudare sette camicie to have a tough time of it

la maglia jersey, top
la maglietta tee-shirt
il maglione sweater
lavorare a maglia to knit

le calze socks
i collant tights
i calzini men's socks
scalzo barefoot

le scarpe shoes
le scarpe da ginnastica trainers
le scarpette da ballo ballet shoes
gli scarponi boots
gli scarponi da sci ski boots

la borsa bag
la borsetta handbag
il borsellino purse
la borsa dell'acqua calda hot-water bottle
la borsa di studio scholarship

la giacca jacket
la giacca a vento anorak

il collo neck
il colletto collar
la collana necklace

la cintura belt
la cintura di sicurezza seabelt

il polso wrist
il polsino cuff
un uomo di polso a man of
   nerve

il vestito dress, suit
il vestito da sera evening gown
il vestito da sposa wedding
   dress
la vestaglia dressing gown

Now complete the following sentences:

22 I signori passeggeri sono pregati di allacciarsi _ _ _ _ _ _ _ _ _ _ _

_ _ _ _ _ _ _ _ _.
Passengers are requested to fasten their seatbelts.

23 - **24** Se farà troppo caldo potremo lavorare senza _ _ _ _ _ _ _ , in _ _ _ _ _ _ _

_ _ _ _ _ _ _ _ _.
*If it is too hot today we'll be able to work without our jacket on,
in shirtsleeves.*

25 - **26** Per favore, bambini, mettetevi un paio di _ _ _ _ _ _ , non girate per

casa _ _ _ _ _ _ _.
*Children, please put a pair of socks on, don't walk around
the house barefoot.*

27 - **28** Si è comprata una _ _ _ _ _ _ _ _ _ _ e due _ _ _ _ _ _ _ _ _ _ _ _ _ _

nuov _.
She bought a dressing gown and two new nightdresses.

29 - **30** Ogni anno l'istituto assegna dieci _ _ _ _ _ _ _ _ _ _ _ _ _ agli studenti

più meritevol _.
*Every year the college awards ten scholarships to the most
deserving students.*

Key points:
Relative pronouns

Do you sometimes hesitate between the relative pronouns **chi** *and* **che**?

Many mistakes are caused because people are influenced by other languages, French in this case, and tend to opt for the word that 'sounds OK'. This chapter will highlight some of the most common areas of error with relative pronouns and suggest some ways to improve your style when using them.

I   *Chi* or *che*?

It is in fact very easy to distinguish between **chi** and **che**: their functions within a sentence are very different.

Chi is used in two cases. The first use is in a question, to mean 'who'. This question can be direct or indirect and **chi** can be preceded by a preposition. For example:

Chi è arrivato prima alla stazione?
[Who arrived first at the station?]
Ti hanno detto chi gli ha scritto?
[Have they told you who has written to them?]
Davvero non so chi sia quel tipo con gli occhiali.
[I really don't know who the guy in the specs is.]
Volevo proprio chiederle con chi era uscita ieri sera.
[I really wanted to ask her who she had gone out with last night.]
Non sa mai per chi compra tutti quei regali, li compra e basta!
[S/he never knows who s/he buys all those presents for, s/he just buys them!]

If you are unsure whether a sentence is an indirect question, see if it hides a direct one. For example:

Non siamo riusciti a scoprire di chi è quell'auto rossa.
[We haven't managed to find out who the owner of that red car is.]

is hiding the question: **di chi è quell'auto rossa?**

Look back at the previous examples: which direct questions are hidden in indirect sentences? Write them down in the box:

---

1 ....

2 ....

3 ....

The second use of **chi** is to refer to two elements in a sentence. When it is used like this, **chi** means 'the person who', 'the people who', 'the one who', 'those who'. Look at these examples:

> **Chi arriva per primo al cinema, aspetterà tutti gli altri.**
> [The person who gets to the cinema first will wait for all the others.]

In this sentence **chi** is the subject both of **arriva** and of **aspetterà**, and so has a dual purpose in the sentence.

> **Non sono molto contento di lavorare con chi fuma tutto il tempo.**
> [I'm not very happy about working with people who smoke all the time.]

In this sentence **chi** is both the object of the preposition **con** and the subject of **fuma**.

Look how **chi** is used to join two sentences together or to shorten longer sentences:

> **In genere non mi va di prestare i miei libri, se non conosco più che bene le persone.**
> **In genere non mi va di prestare i miei libri a chi non conosco più che bene.**
> [I generally don't like lending my books to people I don't know really well.]
> **Gli insegnanti daranno volentieri ulteriori spiegazioni agli studenti, se loro ne avranno bisogno.**
> **Gli insegnanti daranno volentieri ulteriori spiegazioni a chi ne avrà bisogno.**
> [Teachers will be glad to give further explanations to whoever needs them.]

Che, on the other hand, can be used to replace any <u>one</u> noun in a sentence, but only one. The noun it replaces or refers to can be a person, animal or thing, masculine or feminine, singular or plural. It is the most widely used relative pronoun, (and the easiest to use, as it requires no adjustment for gender or number!). The only restriction is that it cannot be used with prepositions.

Look how the following sentences have been joined using **che**:

> **Alla fine ho deciso di comprare la cravatta di seta. A mia moglie piaceva particolarmente una cravatta di seta.**
>
> **Alla fine ho deciso di comprare la cravatta di seta *che* piaceva particolarmente a mia moglie.**
>
> [In the end I decided to buy the silk tie which my wife particularly liked.]
>
> **Per fortuna ho ritrovato le chiavi della macchina. Stamattina avevo perso le chiavi della macchina.**
>
> **Per fortuna ho ritrovato le chiavi della macchina *che* avevo perso stamattina.**
>
> [Luckily I found the car keys that I had lost this morning.]

Join the following sentences, using **che**:

---

4 Quella ragazza coi capelli lunghi e biondi si chiama Laura. Laura sta parlando con Cristiano.

....

....

5 L'altra sera al ristorante ho rivisto un vecchio amico, Paolo. Avevo conosciuto Paolo quando abitavo a Padova.

....

....

6 A volte è sconcertante lavorare con persone ambiziosissime. Le persone troppo ambiziose pensano esclusivamente alla propria carriera.

....

....

Now complete the following passage with **che** or **chi**:

7-**14**   Come passano le loro serate gli italiani? Per rilassarsi e distrarsi, moltissimi scelgono di guardare la televisione, ... non manca ormai in nessuna casa italiana. Con il fenomeno delle TV private, ... è cominciato negli anni Settanta, la televisione ha assunto un'importanza sempre maggiore nella vita degli italiani. Fortunatamente, c'è anche .... preferisce ascoltare la radio o della musica, ... si dedica al proprio passatempo preferito o ai piccoli lavori .... non ha il tempo di svolgere durante il giorno.

     .... abita in città può andare al cinema, a teatro, a un concerto o in qualche locale ad ascoltare la musica o a bere qualcosa. Ovviamente sono i giovani quelli .... escono più spesso, soprattutto nelle serate di venerdì e sabato. Si va a cena fuori e poi al cinema o in discoteca, oppure a casa di amici per mangiare insieme, chiacchierare, giocare. D'estate, poi, si esce sempre la sera, anche soltanto per fare una passeggiata e vedere .... si incontra in giro, prendere un gelato o bere qualcosa di fresco.

II   Using *il che* and *per cui*

Il che is very easy to use and can be quite useful when you need to conclude a sentence concisely, summarizing in one word the idea you have put forward. It refers to the whole preceding sentence, not to just one word in it, and means 'which'. Here are some examples:

Paolo arriva sempre in ritardo, il che è molto seccante per tutti.
[Paolo always arrives late, which is very annoying for everyone.]
L'agenzia di viaggi richiede il pagamento anticipato, il che conferma i nostri sospetti sulla sua serietà.
[The travel agents request payment upfront, which confirms our suspicions about their honesty.]
Mia sorella vuole a tutti i costi andare a vivere da sola, il che significa altre discussioni in famiglia.
[My sister wants to go and live on her own at all costs, which means more arguments at home.]

In all of these sentences, **il che** can be replaced by **e questo** (i.e. **questo fatto, questa cosa, questa situazione**).

Rewrite the following sentences using **il che**:

---

15 **Anche ieri Paolo è arrivato al lavoro in ritardo, ma questo non ha stupito nessuno.**
Yesterday, too, Paolo arrived at work late, but this did not surprise anyone.

....
....

16 **L'Articolo 3 della Costituzione sancisce l'uguaglianza delle donne agli uomini. Questo può sembrare strano, considerata la situazione della maggioranza delle donne italiane.**
Article 3 of the Constitution sanctions the equality of women to men. This may seem strange, considering the situation of the majority of Italian women.

....
....

17 **Il lavoratore italiano non può rinunciare alle ferie. Ciò significa che è obbligato a riposarsi!**
An Italian worker cannot give up his holidays. This means that he's forced to take a rest!

....
....

Per cui can be used to connect two sentences when the second one expresses the outcome or result of what is expressed in the first one. It means 'so', 'therefore'.
Here are some examples:

> **Dobbiamo ancora finire di cenare, per cui per il momento non posso uscire.**
> [We still have to finish our dinner, so for the time being I can't come out.]
> **Non avevano ricevuto la conferma, per cui non hanno inviato il pagamento.**
> [They had not received a confirmation, therefore they did not send the payment.]

In the following sentences, fill the gaps with **il che** or **per cui**:

---

18 All'estero diventiamo perfino più patriottici, ... è tutto dire per un popolo che
ha un vago concetto della patria!

*When abroad, we become even more patriotic, which says it all
about a people which has only a vague idea of homeland!*

19 L'aereo è partito alle dieci meno un quarto, ... dovrebbe essere già qui.

The plane left at a quarter to ten, so it should be here by now.

20 Gli italiani non hanno una tradizione letteraria sui viaggi da loro fatti, ... può
sorprendere, considerando che alcuni fra i più famosi navigatori ed esploratori
furono italiani.

*Italians don't have a tradition of writing about the journeys they
have made, which might be surprising, considering that some of
the most famous navigators and explorers were Italian.*

21 Per molte persone è difficilissimo vivere senza i propri animali, ... rinunciano
addirittura alle vacanze pur di non lasciarli soli.

*For many people it is very difficult to live without their animals, for
which reason they even give up their holidays so as not to leave
them alone.*

22 Il desiderio di chi viaggia è avere esperienze autentiche, ... a volte scelgono
condizioni che noi definiremmo squallide pur di provare il gusto dell'autentico.

*The desire of those who travel is to have authentic experiences,
so they sometimes choose conditions we would call squalid as
long as they experience an authentic flavour.*

III   Using *cui* and *il/la/i/le cui*

Cui always refers to a noun, like **che**, but, unless it means 'whose' (see
below), it is preceded by a preposition.

> **Non tutti hanno letto il libro da cui è stato tratto il film**
> ***Il signore degli anelli.***
>
> [Not everyone has read the book on which the film ***The Lord of
> the Rings*** is based.]
>
> **L'autore di cui abbiamo parlato oggi e con cui si conclud-
> erà la nostra panoramica della narrativa italiana del
> dopoguerra è Alessandro Baricco.**
>
> [The writer about whom we have talked today and with whom we
> shall conclude our overview of postwar Italian fiction is Alessandro
> Baricco.]

Cui can also mean 'whose'. In this case it is placed between the article and the noun it refers to. Look at these examples:

> **I nostri genitori non ci lasciano mai guardare film le cui immagini sono troppo violente.**
> [Our parents never allow us to watch films whose scenes are too violent.]
> **Mia madre dice di aver incontrato molte persone qualunque, la cui vita è però appassionante.**
> [My mother says she has come across many ordinary people, whose lives are nevertheless fascinating.]

Rewrite the following sentences using **il/la/i/le cui**:

23 **Siamo andati a trovare dei nostri amici. La casa di questi nostri amici si trova vicino allo stadio.**
We went to see some friends of ours. The house of these friends of ours is near the football ground.

....
....

24 **Sosteniamo che lo stato debba tutelare tutte le comunità. La lingua di queste comunità è minoritaria.**
We maintain that the state must protect all communities. The language of these communities is a minority one.

....
....

25 **Silvio si è fidanzato con una ragazza. Il padre della ragazza è deputato in Parlamento.**
Silvio has got engaged to a girl. The girl's father is a Member of Parliament.

....
....

26 **Non mi piacciono i ragazzi se i loro capelli hanno troppo gel.**
I don't like boys if their hair has too much gel on it.

....
....

IV   (*Tutto*) *ciò/quello che*

There are two cases in which you will need to use **ciò** or **quello** before the relative pronouns **che** or **cui**:

- to translate 'what' when it means 'the thing(s) which', as in:

  Quello/ciò che mi piace di lui è la sua flemma.
  [What I like about him is his cool/composure.]
  Fammi vedere ciò/quello che hai comprato.
  [Show me what you have bought.]

- after the indefinite pronoun **tutto**, as in:

  Tutto ciò/quello che ti ho detto è vero.
  [Everything (that) I have told you is true.]
  Dobbiamo procurarci tutto ciò di cui avremo bisogno in campeggio.
  [We need to get everything we'll need when camping.]

You need to be particularly careful with this, as in the equivalent English sentence the relative pronoun is normally omitted, but omitting the relative pronoun is not possible in Italian.

Complete the following sentences:

---

27 Ho fatto .... ho potuto per lei.
I have done all I could for her.

28 Avete .... avete bisogno?
Have you got everything you need?

29 .... vorrei veramente fare stasera è andare al cinema.
What I would really like to do this evening is go to the cinema.

30 Non ho capito una parola di .... mi hai detto.
I did not understand a word of what you said.

See for further information
Soluzioni!, Chapter 13
A Reference Grammar of Modern Italian, Chapter 7

Upgrade your vocabulary: Leisure, youth culture and music

DAY 4

Being able to talk and write with confidence, using a wide and appropriate vocabulary about young people's values and interests, is fundamentally important, as well as being an interesting and useful topic. Many of the expressions you'll learn in this chapter are idiomatic, and will serve you well to raise the standard of your Italian.

il/la giovane young person
giovane young
la gioventù youth

il valore (m. see page 6 in Day 1) value
il gusto taste, preference
l'interesse interest
interessarsi di to be interested in
la passione passion
avere la passione di to have a passion for
essere appassionato di to be fond of

il conflitto conflict, clash
conflittuale based on conflict, as in
il rapporto conflittuale, a relationship based on conflict
ribellarsi to rebel
ribelle rebellious
appartenere to belong
la carriera career
fare carriera to have a career

la compagnia/comitiva group of friends
il/la coetaneo/-a person of the same age
trovarsi/incontrarsi to meet, gather

il tempo libero free time
il divertimento amusement
divertirsi to enjoy oneself
il passatempo pastime
lo svago amusement
svagarsi to take one's mind off things
il capriccio whim

l'accordo agreement
andare d'accordo con to get on well with

l'aspetto look, appearance
aspettare to wait for
aspettarsi to expect
l'aspettativa expectation

1 Guess the meaning of **capriccioso:**

....

2 Guess 'disagreement':
il __ __ __ __ __ __ __ __ __ __

3 Guess the meaning of **il conflitto fra le generazioni:**

....

4 Guess the meaning of **il segno di appartenenza:**

....

5 Guess 'rebellion':
la __ __ __ __ __ __ __ __ __ __

6 Guess the meaning of **corrispondere alle aspettative:**

....

7 Guess 'imagination':
l' __ __ __ __ __ __ __ __ __ __ __ __

8 Guess 'to imagine':

__ __ __ __ __ __ __ __ __ __

---

impegnato busy, involved
impegnarsi in to devote oneself to
l'impegno engagement, undertaking
ambizioso ambitious
conformista conformist
maturo mature
disinvolto confident, free-and-easy
altruista altruistic
dinamico dynamic

disimpegnato uninvolved,
    uncommitted

apatico apathetic
indifferente indifferent
anticonformista
    nonconformist
immaturo immature
timido shy
egoista selfish
sedentario sedentary

---

9 Guess the meaning of **egocentrico:**

....

10 Guess 'generous':

__ __ __ __ __ __ __ __ __

11 Guess the meaning of **parlare con disinvoltura:**

....

lo sport sport
sportivo sports (adj.), sporty
giocare a to play a (competitive)
   sport or a game, e.g.
Gioco a calcio I play football
      a tennis tennis
      a pallavolo (**la pallavolo**, f.)
         volleyball
      a pallacanestro
      (**la pallacanestro**, f.) basketball
      a carte cards
      a scacchi chess
      a biliardo pool
      a freccette darts
fare/praticare to play a
   (non-competitive) sport
Faccio nuoto I swim
      equitazione I go horse-riding
      atletica I do athletics
      ginnastica I do gymnastics
      pattinaggio I skate
      il tiro con l'arco I do archery
      ciclismo I cycle
      sci I ski
      aerobica I do aerobics
allenarsi to train

lo stadio ground, stadium
la palestra gym
il campo court (**da tennis**)
la piscina swimming pool
la pista rink
il maneggio riding school

la partita match, game, as in
fare una partita a tennis
   to have a game of tennis

la gara competition, as in
vincere una gara di sci
   to win a skiing competition

la squadra team
far parte di una squadra
   to be in a team
fare il tifo per una squadra
   to support a team

---

12 Guess the meaning of **lo sport di squadra:**
....

13 Guess 'training':
   l'_ _ _ _ _ _ _ _**mento**

14 Guess the meaning of **l'allenatore:**
....

15 Guess the meaning of **i tifosi della squadra nazionale inglese:**
....

la musica classica classical music
    leggera popular music
    barocca Baroque music
    lirica operatic music

il concerto concert
sconcertante disconcerting

l'accordo chord, agreement
accordare to tune
accordarsi to reach agreement
discordante discordant

l'armonia harmony
armonico harmonic
armonizzare to harmonize

l'orchestra orchestra
il direttore d'orchestra conductor

dirigere un'orchestra to
    conduct an orchestra
orchestrare to orchestrate
orchestrale orchestral

il tempo time
a tempo in time
fuori tempo out of time

il tono tone
intonato tuneful

la melodia melody
melodico melodic

il ritmo rhythm
ritmato rhythmical

---

16 Guess the meaning of *stonato:*

....

17 Guess 'harmonious':

— — — — — — — — —

18 Guess 'harmonica':

l' _ _ _ _ _ _ _ _ **a bocca**

---

lo strumento musicale musical
    instrument
suonare uno strumento to play
    an instrument

il quartetto quartet

il violino violin
la viola viola
il violoncello cello
il contrabasso double bass
la tromba trumpet, bugle
il corno horn
il flauto flute

cantare to sing
la canzone song
il coro choir
il complesso group

la chitarra guitar
il basso elettrico electric bass
la batteria drums, drumkit
la tastiera keyboard
il clarino clarinet
l'oboe oboe
il fagotto bassoon

19 Guess the meaning of **la musica corale:**

....

20 Guess 'violinist':
il/la _ _ _ _ _ _ _ _ _ _

21 Guess 'drummer':
il/la _ _ _ _ _ _ _ _ _ _

22 Guess the meaning of **un quintetto d'archi:**

....

---

il compositore composer
comporre compose

registrare to record
il registratore tape recorder
lo stereo hi-fi system

il paroliere lyricist
le parole lyrics

il cantautore/la cantautrice
  singer-songwriter

il successo success, hit

The following need no translation:

il jazz
il blues
il reggae

il rock
il walkman
la musica pop

---

23 Guess the meaning of **una canzone di successo:**

....

24 Guess 'recording':
la _ _ _ _ _ _ _ _ _ _ _ _

25 Guess 'composition':
la _ _ _ _ _ _ _ _ _ _ _ _

Now translate the following sentences into English:

26 - 27 La discoteca è il luogo d'incontro fondamentale per i giovani d'oggi. La danza è l'unico modo per esprimere quello che si è e quello che si prova.

....

....

28 - 29 I 18–24enni sono oggi in Italia i più accaniti frequentatori di cinema, i più assidui ascoltatori di radio private, i più regolari lettori – le donne soprattutto – di stampa periodica.

....

....

30 Hai sentito l'ultimo CD di questo complesso? Il cantante è bravissimo, ma anche il chitarrista, il tastierista e il bassista sono ottimi musicisti.

....

....

Key points: Agreement II – *molto, troppo* and *poco; migliore* vs. *meglio; tutto, ogni, qualche*

DAY 5

*Do you make mistakes with the agreement of words like **molto** and **troppo**? Do you have problems choosing between **meglio** and **migliore**? Are you sometimes unsure about the correct forms of seemingly easy words like **tutto**, **qualche** and **ogni**? The following exercises will help you get your agreements and forms right.*

I Adverb or adjective?

Words like **molto** and **troppo** can be adverbs or adjectives, depending on how they are used in a sentence. As we have seen in Day 1, adjectives must agree in gender (masculine or feminine) and number (singular or plural) with the noun they qualify, while the endings of adverbs never change. First, then, you must be able to tell when **molto**, **troppo** and other words like these (see below for a list) are adverbs.

Adverbs have three possible uses:

*   They modify the meaning of verbs, as in: **Camminiamo *lentamente/ spesso/insieme/molto*.** [We walk *slowly/often/together/very much*.]
*   They modify the meaning of adjectives, as in: **Ho letto un libro *veramente/piuttosto/proprio/molto* interessante**. [I have read a *truly/rather/really/very* interesting book.]
*   They modify the meaning of other adverbs, as in: **Camminiamo *piuttosto/sempre/spesso/molto* lentamente**. [We walk *rather/ always/often/very* slowly.]

Here are some sentences where **molto** and **troppo** are adverbs. Make sure you realize which type of word they modify:

> **Non bevo mai molto la mattina.**
> [I never drink very much in the morning.]
> **Avete speso troppo!**
> [You have spent too much!]
> **Il clima inglese è davvero molto strano!**
> [The English climate is truly very strange!]
> **Questa radio è troppo piccola.**
> [This radio is too small.]

Non usciamo molto spesso con loro.
[We don't go out with them very often.]
Sono arrivati troppo presto.
[They arrived too early.]

As you can see, when **molto** and **troppo** are adverbs, their endings do not change. To help you remember this rule, think of it this way: when it means 'very', **molto** doesn't *vary*.

When words like **molto** and **troppo** modify (or replace) a noun, they are adjectives (or pronouns) and as such they need to agree with that noun, as in:

Faccio molte passeggiate in campagna.
[I take many walks in the countryside.]
In centro c'è sempre molta gente.
[There are always many people in the centre.]
Molti vanno al cinema la domenica.
[Many (people) go to the cinema on Sundays.]
Ho preso troppo sole e mi sono scottata la schiena.
[I caught too much sun and got my back sunburnt.]
La frutta mi piace davvero e ne mangio sempre molta.
[I really like fruit and I always eat lots (of it).]
Non guardo più i film western, ne ho visti troppi da bambina.
[I don't watch westerns anymore, I saw too many of them as a child.]

Be particularly careful when **molto** and **troppo** are pronouns, as in the third, fifth and sixth sentences above. In sentences containing the pronoun **ne, molto** and **troppo** must agree with the noun replaced by **ne** (i.e. **molta frutta** and **troppi film** in the fifth and sixth sentences above).

Here is a table of the words which follow these rules, with their meanings as adverbs and as adjectives:

alquanto	somewhat	some, several
molto	very	much, many
moltissimo	really very	a great deal of
parecchio	rather	a considerable amount, several
poco	not very	not much, not many
pochissimo	very little	very little, very few
tanto	so very	so much, so many
tantissimo	really so very	really so much, so many
troppo	too	too much, too many

In the following sentences, indicate when these words are being used as adverbs by ticking the box(es) at the end of each sentence:

1 - **2** Non bevo mai molto caffé, mi rende troppo nervosa. [ ] [ ]
I never drink too much coffee, it makes me too nervous.

3 - **4** Il bridge è troppo difficile per noi: ci sono troppe regole da ricordare. [ ] [ ]
Bridge is too difficult for us: there are too many rules to remember.

5 - **7** Dopo aver insistito parecchio li ho convinti che eravamo troppo pochi. [ ] [ ] [ ]
After insisting a good deal I convinced them that there were too few of us.

8 - **9** Mi è sembrato un libro alquanto scadente: ne ho letti pochissimi di così deludenti. [ ] [ ]
The book seemed somewhat poor to me: I have read very few of them that have been so disappointing.

In the following sentences, choose the correct form of the words in brackets:

10 - **11** Questa torta ha un sapore (molto/molte) delicato e contiene (pochissimo/pochissimi) grassi.
This cake has a very delicate flavour and it contains very little fat.

12 - **13** Siamo in (troppo/troppi): se prendiamo due macchine staremo (molti/molto) più comodi.
There are too many of us: if we take two cars we'll be much more comfortable.

14 - **15** È stata un'ottima cena: abbiamo speso (poca/poco) e abbiamo assaggiato (parecchio/parecchi) piatti esotici.
It's been an excellent dinner: we didn't spend much and we have tasted several exotic dishes.

16 - **19** Non si vive (molto/molte) bene in questo quartiere: ci sono (tantissimo/tantissimi) edifici e (troppo/troppi) (pochi/poco) alberi.
It's not very good to live in this area: there are so many buildings and too few trees.

II *Migliore* or *meglio*?

A similar distinction to that seen for **molto** applies to **migliore** and **meglio**, and to the other pairs of adjectives and adverbs listed below:

Adjectives		Adverbs	
buono	good	**bene**	well
cattivo	bad	**male**	badly
migliore	better, best	**meglio**	better
peggiore	worse, worst	**peggio**	worse

Once again, adjectives modify (or refer to) nouns while adverbs modify (or refer to) verbs. Look at the following examples:

> **Hai fatto bene a comprare questa macchina, è davvero in buone condizioni.**
> [You were right to buy this car, it's really in good condition.]
> **La fretta è sempre cattiva consigliera: ho fatto il peggior affare della mia vita.**
> [Haste is always a bad adviser: I did the worst deal of my life.]
> **Che noia il balletto: era meglio se stavo a casa!**
> [What a bore the ballet is: it would have been better if I had stayed at home!]
> **Ho preso la medicina che mi ha consigliato il medico, ma mi sento peggio.**
> [I have taken the medicine the doctor advised, but I feel worse.]

Now choose the correct form of the words in brackets:

---

20 Lorna gioca davvero molto (buona/bene) a tennis, di sicuro molto (meglio/migliore) di me.
Lorna plays tennis very well indeed, certainly much better than I do.

21 Riccardo è stato un (buon/bene) amico, di sicuro (migliore/meglio) di Simone.
Richard has been a good friend, certainly better than Simon.

22 Avete (bene/buone) possibilità di vittoria. Vinca il (migliore/meglio)!
You have a good chance of victory. May the best man win!

23 Non hai voluto ascoltare i nostri consigli. (Buone/bene),
(peggio/peggiore) per te!
You have not wanted to listen to our advice. Well, on your head be it!

III   Using *tutto*, *qualche* and *ogni* correctly

When it is an adjective, **tutto** is followed by the article (or a demonstrative) and the noun it refers to and agrees with the noun in gender and number, as in:

tutto il giorno all day	**tutti i giorni** every day
tutto il libro the whole book	**tutti i libri** all of the books, every book
tutta la casa the entire house	**tutte le case** all of the houses, every house

tutto lo spettacolo the whole show
tutto quest'anno this entire year
tutta quella folla all that crowd

tutti gli spettacoli every show, all shows
tutti questi anni all these years
tutte quelle ragazze all those girls

If there is a numeral, this is preceded by **e**, but **tutto** still agrees with the noun, as in:

tutti e due i miei genitori both of my parents
tutti e quattro i libri all four books
tutte e venti le lettere all twenty letters
tutte e cinque queste caramelle all five of these sweets

When **tutto** is a pronoun, it is on its own, as in:

Ho mangiato tutto.
[I have eaten everything.]
Hai letto la lettera? – Sì, l'ho letta tutta.
[Have you read the letter? – Yes, I have read it all.]
Adoro i film di Fellini, li ho visti tutti.
[I love Fellini's films, I have seen them all.]
Sono stufa di queste riviste: le ho già sfogliate tutte.
[I am fed up with these magazines: I have already leafed through them all.]

Ogni and **qualche** are always followed by a singular noun. **Ogni** + singular noun has the same meaning as **tutti/tutte** + article + plural noun, as in:

ogni giorno = tutti i giorni every day
ogni mattina = tutte le mattine every morning

Despite being always followed by a singular noun, the meaning of **qualche** is always plural, as in:

qualche giorno a few days
qualche settimana a few weeks

Complete the following sentences with the correct expression:

24 Vieni a trovarmi .... volte che vuoi.
Come and see me every time you like.

25 .... volta vado in piscina.
I sometimes go swimming.

26 .... queste tovaglie sono state ricamate.
All these table cloths have been embroidered.

27 .... volta che la vedo ha una pettinatura diversa.
Every time I see her she has a different hairstyle.

28 Conosci ....?
Do you know everybody?

29 Ho letto .... i suoi libri.
I have read all four of his books.

30 .... critiche che hanno ricevuto sono state ingiuste.
All the criticism they have received has been unfair.

See for further information
Soluzioni!, Chapters 4, 5 and 12
A Reference Grammar of Modern Italian, Chapters 6.38, 9, 13 and 16

Upgrade your vocabulary: Mass media – TV, press and cinema

DAY 6

Media communication and media culture are hot topics everywhere. A good degree of competence and accuracy when talking or writing about these issues will add value and style to your Italian.

i mezzi di comunicazione di massa mass media
comunicare to communicate (note that all words derived from **comune** are spelt with one 'm')

la televisione/la TV (**tivù**) TV
la televisione di stato state TV
     privata commercial TV
     via satellite satellite TV
     via cavo cable TV
la rete/l'emittente televisiva TV network

la trasmissione broadcast
 in diretta live
 in differita/registrata pre-recorded
trasmettere to broadcast
registrare to record
andare in onda to be on air
l'onda wave
la puntata episode
l'indice (m.) **d'ascolto** ratings
l'indice index
il canone TV licence fee

la radio radio
radiofonico radio (adj.)
il canale televisivo TV channel

il programma programme
programmare to plan

la telenovela TV soap
il teleromanzo TV novel
lo sceneggiato TV drama
la scena scene, stage
il varietà variety show
la pubblicità advertising
l'attualità current affairs

lo spettatore viewer
il presentatore
la presentatrice presenter

1 Guess the meaning of **mandare in onda:**

....

2 Guess 'VCR (video recorder)':
 il _

3 Guess the meaning of **il telequiz:**

....

4 Guess the meaning of **lo sceneggiato a puntate:**

....

5 Guess 'to introduce':

— — — — — — — — — —

6 Guess the meaning of **lo spot pubblicitario:**

....

7 Guess 'a current affairs programme':
un _ _ _ _ _ _ _ _ _ **d'** _ _ _ _ _ _ _ _ _

8 Guess the meaning of **la cultura di massa:**

....

---

la stampa press
stampare to print
il giornale/quotidiano
  newspaper, daily
la rivista/il periodico magazine
settimanale weekly
mensile monthly
la testata heading, newspaper
il titolo title, headline, credit, as in
i titoli di coda closing credits
sfogliare to leaf through
la foglia leaf (of tree)
il foglio sheet (of paper)
l'inserto supplement
la notizia piece of news

l'informazione
  (f. – see page 6 in Day 1)
  (piece of) information
informare to inform
l'articolo article
l'articolo di fondo editorial
la cronaca local news
il/la cronista reporter
la rubrica column
l'inchiesta/il servizio report
l'inviato correspondent
il redattore editor
la redazione draft (of article),
  editorial office

---

9 Guess the meaning of **l'opinione pubblica:**

....

10 Guess 'sport column':
la _ _ _ _ _ _ _ _ _ _ _ _ _ _

11 Guess the meaning of **un settimanale femminile di moda:**

....

il cinema cinema (place and genre)
Che cosa dànno al cinema?
   What's on at the movies?
la sala cinematografica movie
   theatre
il cinema muto silent films
il cinema parlato talkies
il cinema d'autore art house films

il/la divo/-a/la stella del cinema
   film star
la controfigura double

girare un film to shoot a film
il regista director
dirigere to direct
la regia direction

la sceneggiatura screenplay
il copione script
copiare to copy
la trama plot

il successo success
il successo d'incassi box-office hit
avere successo to be successful

lo schermo screen
il grande schermo the big
   screen, cinema
il piccolo schermo the small
   screen, TV
doppiare to dub
i sottotitoli subtitles

interpretare un ruolo to play
   a part
l'interprete performer,
   interpreter
recitare to act

la colonna sonora soundtrack
la musica di sottofondo
   background music
la sequenza sequence
l'inquadratura frame

**un film vietato ai minori di
   18 anni** film rated '18'

la censura censorship
censurare to censor

---

12 Guess the meaning of **la multisala:**
....

13 Guess 'to subtitle':
   — — — — — — — — — — — —

14 Guess the meaning of **tramare:**
....

15 Guess the meaning of **un successo di critica e di pubblico:**
....

16 Guess 'performance':
   l'_ _ _ _ _ _ _ _ _ _ _ _ _ _ _ _ _

17 Guess the meaning of **la scuola di recitazione:**
....

un film d'avventura adventure film
    di animazione animation
    di fantascienza science fiction
    dell'orrore horror
    di spionaggio spy
    giallo thriller
    poliziesco detective

18 Guess the meaning of **un film d'azione:**
....

19 Guess the meaning of **un film epico:**
....

20 Guess the meaning of **un film musicale:**
....

21 Guess 'a dramatic film':
un __ __ __ __   __ __ __ __ __ __ __ __ __ __

22 Guess the meaning of **un film sentimentale:**
....

23 Guess the meaning of **i cartoni animati:**
....

Now translate the following sentences into English:

24 – 27 Metà comico, metà tragico; metà divertente, metà toccante: il primo film anche drammatico di Roberto Benigni è due film distinti. Le due parti rimangono divise, il film non è pienamente riuscito ma è il migliore che Benigni abbia sinora diretto, e lui è un protagonista bravissimo.
....
....

28 – 30 Il linguaggio della pubblicità non solo deve colpire l'attenzione, ma deve essere facile da ricordare; in altre parole, questo linguaggio deve essere soprattutto espressivo.
....
....

Key points:
Expressions of time

Do you have problems translating the word 'time' into Italian? Do you hesitate when choosing a preposition in an expression of time? This chapter will look in detail at the options for the word 'time' and at various tricky time expressions.

I Time

VOLTA (occasion)
una volta, due volte, tre volte once, twice, three times
questa volta this time   **la prima volta** the first time
qualche volta sometimes   **l'ultima volta** the last time
un'altra volta another time,   **ancora una volta** once again
    next time   **di volta in volta** from time to time
a volte at times

Also note the following expressions:

una volta tanto once in a while
per volta at a time, e.g. **Facciamo una cosa per volta, altrimenti
   ci confondiamo.** Let's do one thing at a time, otherwise we'll get
   mixed up.
C'era una volta Once upon a time there was

MOMENTO (point in time)
in qualsiasi momento at   **in quel momento** at that time
   any time   (then)
in questo momento at this   **da un momento all'altro** any
   time (now)   time now
al momento giusto/sbagliato **non è il momento di** ... this is
   at the right/wrong time   not the time to
per il momento for the time
   being

TEMPO
(a) length of time; time as general phenomenon
aver tempo di fare qualcosa to have time to do something
perdere tempo to waste time
tutto il tempo (for) the whole time
nel giro di poco tempo within a short space of time
(b) right time for
arrivare in tempo per to arrive in time to

(c) period (usually in the past)
a quei tempi in those days
di questi tempi these days
in tempo di guerra in wartime
ai miei tempi in my days

ORA, ORARIO (time relating to hour of the day or to timetables)
Che ore sono? What time is it?
Hai l'ora esatta? Do you have the right time?
È ora di andare It's time to go
domani a quest'ora this time tomorrow
Era ora! About time!
l'ora di punta the rush hour
l'ora di pranzo lunchtime
l'orario d'uffico, di lavoro, delle lezioni office, work, school hours
l'orario di apertura/chiusura opening/closing times
in orario on time, according to the timetable

Fill the gaps in the following sentences using the correct expression from the list above:

1 Carla va in palestra .... alla settimana.
Carla goes to the gym three times a week.

2 Non dovreste navigare sull'Internet durante .... di lavoro.
You shouldn't surf the net in company time.

3 Ci vogliono .... e pazienza per imparare bene una lingua.
It takes time and patience to learn a language well.

4 Sono arrivati appena .... per l'inizio del film.
They arrived just in time for the beginning of the film.

5 Anche lei è di cattivo umore, ...
She too is in a bad mood, sometimes.

6 Il presente è .... migliore per cominciare.
The present is the best time to start.

7 Scusami, non posso proprio restare a cena. ...., magari.
Sorry, I really cannot stay to dinner. Another time, perhaps.

8 .... pochi sapevano leggere e scrivere.
In those days, few people could read and write.

9 Mi avrà chiesto mille .... di andare a trovarla.
She must have asked me a thousand times to go and see her.

10 Si sono conosciuti a gennaio e poco .... dopo si sono sposati.
They met in January and shortly afterwards they got married.

11 Che .... fai? Mi si è fermato l'orologio.
What time do you make it? My watch has stopped.

12 Ha lavorato presso un giornale per qualche ....
He worked at a newspaper for some time.

II Prepositions with expressions of time: 'for', 'in'

If 'for' indicates an intended or an actual period of time, you must use **per**. For example:

Andremo in Italia per due settimane.
[We are going to Italy for two weeks.]
Ha lavorato nello stesso ufficio per molti anni.
[He worked in the same office for many years.]
È stato via per sei mesi.
[He has been away for six months.]
Dovranno chiudere la biblioteca per tutta l'estate.
[They will have to close the library for the whole summer.]
Andiamo a sciare per Natale?
[Shall we go skiing for Christmas?]

If 'for' indicates a period of time up to a present or past moment, you must use **da**. In these cases, the Italian verb will always be in the present and imperfect tense respectively. For example:

Abito in questo appartamento da cinque anni.
[I have been living in this flat for five years.]
Li conosciamo da anni.
[We have known them for years.]
Non si parlano da una settimana.
[They haven't spoken for a week.]

Mi ha detto che fumava da più di trent'anni.
[He told me he had been smoking for more than thirty years.]
Lo sapevate che non andava a scuola da molti giorni?
[Did you know he had not gone to school for many days?]
Frequentavano la stessa palestra da almeno un anno.
[They had been going to the same gym for at least a year.]

Compare these two sets of sentences:

Frequento questa università da un anno.
[I have been attending this university for a year.]
Frequento questa università per un anno.
[I am attending this university for a year.]
Lavoravo in ospedale da un mese.
[I had been working in a hospital for a month.]
Ho lavorato in ospedale per un mese.
[I worked in a hospital for a month.]

Fill the gaps in the following sentences with **per** or **da**, as appropriate:

13 Ho esitato .... qualche secondo prima di rispondere.
I hesitated for a few seconds before answering.

14 È incollato alla televisione .... più di un'ora.
He has been glued to the telly for more than an hour.

15 Perché non andiamo in campagna .... il fine-settimana?
Why don't we go to the country for the weekend?

16 Fermatevi da noi .... qualche giorno!
Stay with us for a few days!

17 Marco aspetta la sua ragazza .... almeno mezz'ora.
Marco has been waiting for his girlfriend for at least half an hour.

18 Cecilia ha aspettato dal dentista .... almeno mezz'ora.
Cecilia waited at the dentist's for at least half an hour.

If 'in' indicates the length of time that something will take, you must use **in**. For example:

Ho letto questo libro in un giorno.
[I read this book in a day.]
Mangiava una tavoletta di cioccolata in tre secondi.
[S/he would eat a bar of chocolate in three seconds.]
Sono capaci di arredare tutta una casa in due giorni.
[They are able to furnish a whole house in two days.]

If 'in' indicates a deadline, the 'time at the end of which', you must use **fra**. For example:

> **L'autobus arriverà fra cinque minuti.**
> [The bus will arrive in five minutes.]
> **Torno fra un minuto.**
> [I'll be back in a minute.]
> **Fra tre settimane comincia la campagna elettorale.**
> [The election campaign begins in three weeks.]

Compare these two sentences:

> **Ti spiego tutto in un minuto.**
> [I'll explain everything in a minute (i.e. it will take me a minute to explain everything).]
> **Ti spiego tutto fra un minuto.**
> [I'll explain everything in a minute (i.e. in a minute's time I'll start to explain).]

Also note the following expressions:

nel 2005 in 2005	**negli anni Novanta** in the nineties
nel ventesimo secolo in the twentieth century	**alle due del pomeriggio** at two in the afternoon
di/la mattina in the morning/s	**a gennaio** in January
d'estate/inverno in the summer/winter	**durante il giorno** in the daytime

In the following sentences, add the missing preposition:

19 Credi davvero che riusciremo a cambiare la ruota .... dieci minuti?
Do you really think that we'll be able to change the wheel in ten minutes?

20 Sarò pronta .... un minuto.
I'll be ready in a minute.

21 Erano in ritardo, ma si sono vestiti .... un batter d'occhio.
They were late, but they got dressed in a flash.

22 .... la notte è nevicato.
It snowed in the night.

23 La rappresentazione comincerà alle sette .... sera.
The performance will begin at seven in the evening.

III   Day, morning, evening, year

Do you find it difficult to decide whether to use **giorno**, **mattina**, **sera**, **anno** or **giornata**, **mattinata**, **serata**, **annata**? The distinction is often one of style, but the words in the second group emphasize the length of time or the events that take place within it. For example:

Buongiorno! Good day!	**Buona giornata!** Have a good day!
gli anni della guerra the war years	**un vino d'annata** a vintage wine
tre sere fa three evenings ago	**una serata piacevole** a pleasant evening

Complete the following sentences with the appropriate word:

24 È stato/a un/un' .... pessimo/a per l'agricoltura.
It's been an awful year for farming.

25 Quello che mi chiedi rappresenta un/una .... di lavoro.
What you are asking me represents a whole day's work.

26 Una .... siamo andati ad un concerto rock con i nostri figli.
One evening we went to a rock concert with our kids.

27 La riunione si terrà in ....
The meeting will take place in the course of the morning.

28 Grazie per la bellissima ....: ci siamo davvero divertiti.
Thanks for the lovely evening: we really enjoyed it.

Now translate the following sentences into Italian:

29 I've been thinking about it for a long time: I'll do it in a minute.
....

30 I thought about it for a long time: I can do it in a minute.
....

See for further information

Soluzioni!, Chapters 15 and 17
A Reference Grammar of Modern Italian, Chapters 11 and 21

Upgrade your vocabulary: Literature and visual arts

Talking about literature and art can appear daunting, but it can be fairly straightforward, provided you know some basic vocabulary. Some of it overlaps with general descriptive vocabulary, so you can use what you learnt on Day 2 about describing people when talking about literary characters, for instance. Being confident and competent when talking or writing about more abstract concepts will definitely raise the standard of your Italian and gain you those all-important extra marks.

la letteratura literature
il/la letterato/-a scholar
letterario literary
letterale literal

la narrativa fiction
la narrazione story
narrare to tell a story
il narratore/la narratrice narrator

il capitolo chapter
capitolare to surrender, give in
ricapitolare to recap, to sum up

la pagina page
voltar pagina to turn over the page

l'argomentazione argument (element of reasoning, NOT 'quarrel' = **la discussione**)
argomentare to argue, to reason (NOT 'to quarrel' = discutere)
l'argomento topic, subject (see also Day 28)

l'epilogo epilogue, conclusion, dénouement
riepilogare to sum up, summarize

---

1 Guess the meaning of **la critica letteraria:**
....

2 Guess 'literally':
— — — — — — — — — — — — —

3 Guess 'dialogue':
il — — — — — — —

4 Guess 'monologue':
il — — — — — — — —

il romanzo novel
il/la romanziere/-a novelist
romanzesco fictional, fantastic

romanzato romanticized
romanticismo romanticism

---

5 Guess the meaning of **un romanzo rosa:**

....

6 Guess 'romantic':

— — — — — — — — — **-a**

7 Guess the meaning of **un romanzo giallo:**

....

8 Guess the meaning of **un romanzo d'amore:**

....

As with **un romanzo giallo**, many of the expressions you learnt in Day 6 to describe types of film can also be used to describe types of novel. Make a list of the ones that interest you.

la persona person
il personaggio character, famous person
la personificazione personification
il personale staff, personnel

il racconto story, tale, short story
raccontare (una storia, una bugìa, una barzelletta) to tell (a story, a lie, a joke)

la novella short story
la favola fairy tale, fable

il/la protagonista protagonist, hero/ine

la morale moral, morality, morale, as in
essere su/giù di morale to be feeling cheerful/down
moralista moralistic
immorale immoral

la leggenda legend
leggendario legendary

---

9 Guess the meaning of **un personaggio del mondo sportivo:**

....

10 Guess 'fabulous':

— — — — — — — —

la poesia poetry, poem
il poema poem (particularly epics and very long items of poetry)
la poetica poetics

poetico poetic(al)
il poeta/la poetessa poet
la rima rhyme

---

11 Guess to rhyme with:

— — — — — —   — — —

12 Guess the meaning of **l'onomatopea:**

....

13 Guess the meaning of **onomatopeico:**

....

14 Guess 'assonance' (think of other words ending in -nce, e.g. science **la scienza**)
l'_ _ _ _ _ _ _ _ _

15 Guess the meaning of **l'allitterazione:**

....

---

il ritmo rhythm

la strofa stanza
il verso verse, line of poetry

la sillaba syllable
sillabico syllabic

il simbolo symbol

---

16 Guess 'rhythmic':

— — — — — — — —

17 Guess the meaning of **l'endecasillabo:**

....

18 Guess 'symbolic', 'symbolism', 'symbolist':

— — — — — — — —
il _ _ _ _ _ _ _ _ _ _
il/la _ _ _ _ _ _ _ _ _ _ _

Many more words referring to literary movements, like **il realismo**, **il modernismo**, **l'ermetismo**, **il surrealismo**, will follow the same pattern, so you can easily guess the related forms in -*ist*.

The next set of words relates to theatre and drama:

la commedia comedy
comico comic(al)
la commedia musicale musical
il/la comico/-a comedian/
  comedienne
il/la commediografo/-a
  comedy writer

il teatro theatre
andare a teatro to go to the theatre
l'opera/il lavoro teatrale play

rappresentare to play, perform,
  represent
la rappresentazione performance,
  portrayal
il/la rappresentante representative
interpretare/recitare to play (a part)
il ruolo/la parte part

la tragedia tragedy
tragico tragic
il dramma drama, tragedy
il/la drammaturgo/-a
  playwright
il melodramma melodrama
drammatizzare to (over)
  dramatize
sdrammatizzare to play down

la scena scene
in scena on stage
il palcoscenico stage
lo scenario the set, backdrop
le quinte the wings
dietro le quinte behind the
  scenes

la prima opening night
il debutto debut
debuttare to make one's
  debut

Now complete the following sentences with the missing words:

19 Il _ _ _ _ _ _ _ _ _ di Amleto è uno dei brani shakespeariani più famosi.
Hamlet's monologue is one of the most famous Shakespearean passages.

20 Il Teatro Stabile di Torino metterà _ _ _ _ _ _ _ 'Il gioco delle parti' di Pirandello.
Turin's Repertory Theatre will stage Pirandello's The Rules of the Game.

21 Prima di arrivare al successo, molti _ _ _ _ _ _ d'avanguardia recitano sui palcoscenici dei cabaret.
Before being successful, many avant-garde comedians appear in cabaret.

The last set of words refers to visual arts:

la pittura painting
il pittore/la pittrice painter
dipingere to paint
il pennello paintbrush
la tela canvas
il quadro picture

il ritratto portrait
l'aquarello watercolour
l'acquaforte etching
lo schizzo sketch

la fotografia photography, photograph
fare una fotografia to take a photo
il/la fotografo/-a photographer
fotografare to photograph

l'esposizione exhibition
esporre to exhibit

la scultura sculpture
lo scultore/la scultrice sculptor
scolpire to sculpt
lo scalpello chisel
il marmo marble
la statua statue

incidere to engrave, to record (a song, a record)
l'incisione engraving, recording

disegnare to draw
il disegno drawing

l'inquadratura frame
il primo piano close-up

in bianco e nero black and white
a colori in colour

la pinacoteca art gallery

---

22 Guess 'photogenic':

———————————

23 Guess 'photomontage':
il ————————————————

24 Guess the meaning of **la pennellata:**
....

25 Guess the meaning of **la videoteca:**
....

26 Guess 'portrait artist':
il/la ————————————————

27 Guess 'water-colourist':
l' ————————————————

28 Guess the meaning of **ritrarre:**
....

29 Guess the meaning of **la macchina fotografica:**
....

30 Guess the meaning of **la pittura a olio:**
....

*Are you sometimes unsure about the use of **piacere?** Do the errors you make involve the pronouns and the other words used with **piacere?** This chapter will look in detail at the trickier areas of usage of **piacere** and other impersonal verbs.*

I   *Piace* or *piacciono?*

Unlike the English verb to like, **piacere** is constructed impersonally: instead of saying 'I like this town', you need to say the equivalent of 'This town is pleasing to me', so the thing or things liked become the subject of the Italian construction. In most cases, then, you will need to use either **piace** or **piacciono**: use **piace** if the thing liked is a singular noun or a verb; use **piacciono** if more than one thing – i.e. more than one singular noun or a plural noun – is liked. Here are some examples:

> **La musica italiana mi piace molto.**
> [I like Italian music very much.]
> **Ti piace cantare?**
> [Do you like singing?]
> **L'opera e il teatro mi piacciono molto.**
> [I like opera and theatre very much.]
> **Queste canzoni mi piacciono molto.**
> [I like these songs very much.]

In the following sentences, choose between **piace** and **piacciono**:

1 - **2**	Le piace/piacciono viaggiare? Sì, mi piace/piacciono moltissimo.
	Do you like travelling? Yes, I like it very much.
3	I viaggi esotici piace/piacciono ormai a molti italiani.
	Many Italians now like exotic trips.
4	A chi non piace/piacciono uscire con gli amici o fare una bella festa?
	Who doesn't like going out with friends or having a nice party?
5	Scusami, le uova sode proprio non mi piace/piacciono.
	Sorry, I really don't like hard-boiled eggs.
6	La spesa, i lavori di casa, cucinare: assolutamente non mi piace/piacciono!
	Shopping, housework, cooking: I really dislike them!

Note: as what one likes is the subject of the Italian construction, you don't need a direct object pronoun ('it' 'them' in sentences 1–2 and 6).

II   Which pronoun?

When using **piacere**, several types of sentence are possible, depending on whether the speaker wants to stress the idea of liking, what one likes or the person who likes. In the first two cases, you will need to use the unstressed indirect object pronouns: **mi**, **ti**, **gli**, **le**, **ci**, **vi**. The pronoun you must NEVER use is **si**.

If you are stressing the notion of liking, the sentences will be constructed like this:

> **Vi piace lo sport? Sì, ci piace.**
> [Do you like sport? Yes, we do.]
> **Non ti piace sciare? No, non (mi piace) molto.**
> [Don't you like skiing? No, not much.]
> **Le piacciono gli sport violenti? No, (non mi piacciono) per niente.**
> [Do you like violent sports? No, not at all.]
> **Piace la birra inglese a Paolo? Sì, (gli piace) molto.**
> [Does Paolo like English beer? Yes, (he likes it) very much.]
> **Piacciono le città inglesi a Luisa? Sì, (le piacciono) molto.**
> [Does Luisa like English cities? Yes, (she likes them) very much.]

If you are stressing what you like, the sentences will be similar to these:

> **Che cosa vi piacerebbe fare domenica? Ci piacerebbe soprattutto dormire!**
> [What would you like to do on Sunday? Above all, we would like to sleep!]
> **Quali tipi di musica non vi piacciono? Non ci piace l'opera, per esempio.**
> [What kinds of music don't you like? We don't like opera, for example.]
> **Quali film piacciono di più a Michela? Le piacciono di più i film americani.**
> [Which films does Michela like best? She likes American films best.]
> **Come ti piace il tè? (Mi piace) leggero e senza latte.**
> [How do you like your tea? (I like it) weak and without milk.]

Compare these two sentences:

> **Ti piace il mio vestito nuovo? Sì, moltissimo!**
> [Do you like my new dress? Yes, very much!]

Quale vestito ti piace di più? Quello rosso.
[Which dress do you like best? The red one.]

Using the translation to help you, fill the gaps in the following sets of sentences with the correct form of **piacere** and the correct pronoun:

---

7 – **8** Ragazzi, ... andare in discoteca stasera? Perché no, ottima idea!
Guys, would you like to go to a disco tonight? Why not, excellent idea!

In quale discoteca vi piacerebbe andare? Non importa, ... tutte.
Which disco would you like to go to? It doesn't matter, we like them all.

9 – **10** È vero che a tuo fratello il mare non piace? È vero, non ....
per niente.
Is it true that your brother does not like the seaside? It's true, he doesn't like it at all.

Che cosa non gli piace del mare? Mah, tutto: il caldo, la sabbia.
Non .... neanche i bagni!
What does he not like about the seaside? Well, everything: the heat, the sand. He doesn't even like going for a swim!

11 – **12** Le piace viaggiare, signor Rossi? Certo che mi piace, ...
moltissimo!
Do you like travelling, Mr Rossi? Of course I do, I like it very much!

In quale periodo dell'anno Le piace viaggiare? In primavera, i viaggi
primaverili .... veramente.
At what time of the year do you like travelling? In the spring, I really like springtime trips.

Now answer the following questions as suggested, using **piacere** and the correct pronoun:

---

13 Marco, ti piacerebbe venire a cena da noi domani? (Yes, very much.)
....

14 È vero che non vi piace la casa di Paola? (No, not true, we do.)
....

---

15 Quale dei miei cd ti piace di più? (I like them all!)

....

16 A tua sorella non piacciono i vestiti scuri, vero? (True, she doesn't.)

....

If you want to stress the person who does the liking, you will need to use the stressed object pronouns, with the preposition **a: a me, a te, a lui, a lei, a noi, a voi, a loro**. A similar construction will be used if the person is described by a noun, rather than by a pronoun. Here are some examples:

> **La cioccolata piace a tutti, vero? No, a me non piace.**
> [Everybody likes chocolate, don't they? No, I don't like it.]
> **A chi non piace il calcio? A noi non piace. Neanche ai miei amici piace. A lui, invece, piace moltissimo!**
> [Who does not like football? We don't. Neither do my friends. He, on the contrary, likes it very much!]
> **Anche se a te questo genere di libri può non piacere, ad altri piace molto.**
> [Although you may not like this kind of book, others like it very much.]
> **Vedrai che il nostro regalo piacerà anche ai tuoi genitori.**
> [You'll see, even your parents will like our present.]

In the following sentences, add the missing preposition and pronoun:

17 Ma a voi piace davvero questa tappezzeria? No, ... non piace. Piaceva tanto a nostra nonna.
Do you really like this wallpaper? No, we don't. Our Gran liked it a lot.

18 Mi hanno detto che a Paolo non piace più la bicicletta. No, è a sua moglie che non piace. ... . piace ancora molto.
I've heard that Paolo does not like cycling any more. No, it's his wife who doesn't (like it). He still likes it a lot.

19 A nessuno di noi piacciono i funghi, solo ai miei genitori: ... . piacciono da matti!
None of us likes mushrooms, only my parents do: they are mad about them!

20 Andiamo a vedere Il signore degli anelli? Guarda, ... questo genere di film non piace proprio, ma se piace a te, andiamoci!
Shall we go and see The Lord of the Rings? Look, I really don't like this kind of film, but if you do, let's go!

III   Using *piacere* in compound tenses

In compound tenses, **piacere** and all impersonal verbs like it (see below) use **essere** as their auxiliary. Look at the following examples:

> **Vi è piaciuto il film? Sì, ci è piaciuto molto.**
> [Did you like the film? Yes, we liked it a lot.]
> **È piaciuto il concerto a Paolo? Sì, gli è piaciuto abbastanza.**
> [Did Paolo like the concert? Yes, he liked it well enough.]
> **Che cosa le è piaciuto particolarmente del museo? Le è piaciuta di più la sezione contemporanea.**
> [What did she particularly like about the museum? She liked the contemporary section best.]
> **Speriamo che la cena sia piaciuta a tutti! Ma certo, è piaciuta anche a chi non aveva fame!**
> [Let's hope they all liked the dinner! But of course they did; even those who weren't hungry liked it!]

Re-write the following sentences, putting **piacere** into its compound form:

---

21 Vi piace la mia festa?

....

22 Scusami, i frutti di mare proprio non mi piacciono.

....

23 A chi non piacerebbe fare una bella vacanza?

....

24 Penso che a nessuno piaccia il suo comportamento.

....

25 Piacerà alla mamma quel ristorante? E chi lo sa?

....

IV   Other verbs like *piacere*

Several other verbs are used just like **piacere**. These are the most useful:

bastare	to be enough	**mancare**	to lack, to be missing
convenire	to be advisable	**restare**	to be left
dispiacere	to be sorry	**rimanere**	to be left
interessare	to interest	**servire**	to be useful, to be needed
occorrere	to be needed		

Here are some examples:

> **Ti bastano i soldi? Se no, pago io.**
> [Do you have enough money? If not, I'll pay.]

Non preoccuparti, mi bastano.
[Don't worry, I have enough.]
Dice che un mese di vacanza non gli è bastato.
[He says that a month's holiday wasn't enough for him.]
Gli mancava molto la famiglia, così è tornato in Italia.
[He missed his family a lot, so he's gone back to Italy.]
A chi mancano le fotocopie? A me, ma mi manca solo il primo foglio.
[Who is missing the photocopies? I am, but only the first sheet.]
Mi restano solo più due cioccolatini: chi li vuole?
[I have just two chocolates left: who wants them?]
Le sono rimaste solo due sterline: non le bastano a comprare il libro che vuole.
[She only has two pounds left: it is not enough to buy the book she wants.]
Mi servirebbe una penna nera. Ti dispiace prestarmi la tua?
[I could do with a black pen. Do you mind lending me yours?]
La politica non interessa più ai giovani.
[Young people are no longer interested in politics.]

Translate the following sentences into Italian, using the suggested verbs:

26 Will a week be enough for you to finish the job? **(bastare)**

27 Will we need the dictionary during the exam? **(servire)**

28 He had better talk to his teacher about it. **(convenire)**

29 Nobody is interested in your problems. **(interessare)**

30 If you go abroad, who will you miss most? **(mancare)**

See for further information
Soluzioni!, pages 85, 141, 261–4, 229, 248, 286
A Reference Grammar of Modern Italian, pages 232, 264, 356, 366

Upgrade your vocabulary: Dates and history

Do you hesitate or slow down when you need to use dates or numbers in Italian? Do you make mistakes when you need to write dates or read them aloud? Today's first exercise is designed to increase your confidence and accuracy when using dates and numbers.

First of all, make sure you know the following expressions (note that names of days and months are written with small letters), as well as cardinal and ordinal numbers:

Quanti ne abbiamo oggi? What's the date today?
Oggi ne abbiamo otto. Today's the eighth.

Qual è la data di oggi? What's today's date?
Oggi è il ventidue luglio. Today is 22 July.

Che giorno è oggi? What day is it today?
Oggi è domenica. Today is Sunday.

Sono nato/-a mercoledì primo aprile, millenovecentosettantacinque.
I was born on Wednesday 1 April 1975.

È successo nel milleottocentododici/nel diciannovesimo secolo/nell'Ottocento/a novembre/di martedì.
It happened in 1812/in the nineteenth century/in the 1800s/in November/on a Tuesday.

Dal millenovecentoquindici al millenovecentodiciotto.
From 1915 to 1918.

Entro il quindici ottobre.
By 15 October.

Riccardo III (terzo)
Richard III

Nel quarto secolo a.C. (avanti Cristo)/d.C. (dopo Cristo).
In the fourth century BC/AD

Now do the following exercise orally and time yourself. Say aloud in Italian:

---

1 Today is Monday, 2 July 2004

2 I was born on 8 June 1974, on a Saturday

3 London, 11 May 1965

4 Thursday, 25 December 1778

5 It happened on 1 February 1693

6 In 639 BC

7 Henry VIII

8 Elizabeth II

9 From 1939 to 1945

10 By 31 March 2005

I   Speed and confidence

If you have managed to complete the exercise correctly in under two minutes, your speed is good. For more practice, try repeatedly opening a large diction- ary at random and saying the page number in Italian as fast as you can; or pressing the number keys of your calculator at random with your eyes closed, then opening your eyes and reading out the number displayed in Italian. Do this until you are satisfied that your speed in Italian is close to English.

II   Accuracy

Write out in words the answers you gave for the exercise above. Score one point for each completely correct answer.

---

1 ....

2 ....

3 ....

4 ....

5 ....

6	....
7	....
8	....
9	....
10	....

III Historical vocabulary

The rest of today's work is based on word-groups that you could find useful when dealing with historical subjects. As historical and political vocabulary can overlap, you will have a chance to learn and practise the latter in Day 18.

In the following exercise, see how many of the gaps you can fill without looking up the answers. Score one point if you can fill all the gaps in a group and half a point if not all gaps are filled correctly. When you have done your best from your existing knowledge, and have calculated your score, fill the remaining gaps by consulting the answer section.

11 From **la guerra** *war*

        il/la guerr_ _ _ _ _/**-a** 'warrior'

        la guerr_ _ _ _ _ _ 'guerrilla war(fare)'

        il/la guerr_ _ _ _ _ _ _/**-a** 'guerrilla fighter'

        Guess the meaning of **Guerre stellari** ....

12 From **l'impero** *empire*

        _**mp** _ _ _ _ _ _ _ 'imperial'

        _**mp** _ _ _ _ _ _ _ 'to rule, prevail'

        _**mp** _ _ _ _ _ _ _ 'prevailing' (adj.)

        _**mp** _ _ _ _ _ _ _ 'imperious'

        l'_**mp** _ _ _ _ _ _ _ _ 'emperor'

        l'_**mp** _ _ _ _ _ _ _ _ _ 'empress'

        l'_**mp** _ _ _ _ _ _ _ _ _ _ 'imperialism'

13 From **l'età** *age*

        l'_ _ _ _ **dell'**_ _ _ _ 'the Golden Age'

        l'_ _ _ _ **del** _ _ _ _ _ _ 'Bronze Age'

        l'_ _ _ _ **della** _ _ _ _ _ _ 'Stone Age'

        _ _ _ **eta**_ _ _ _ 'person of the same age'

        la _ _ _ _ _ _ **età** 'the third age, old age'

        la _ _ _ _ _ **'età** 'middle age' BUT **il Medioevo** 'the Middle Ages'

14 From **la vittoria** 'victory'

__ __ __ __ __ __ __ __ __ __ 'victorious'

From **vincere** 'to win'

__ __ **vinc**__ __ __ __ __ 'invincible'

il vinc__ __ __ __ __ __/**la vinc** __ __ __ __ __ __ winner

vinc__ __ __ __ 'winning' (adj.)

15 From **il re** (plur. **i re**) 'king'

re__ __ __ 'royal, real'

re __ __ __ __ __ 'to reign'

re __ __ __ __ __ __ 'reigning' (adj.)

il Re__ __ __ __ **U** __ __ __ __ __ 'the United Kingdom'

la __ __ __ __ __ __ __ 'queen'

16 From **povero, nobile** and **libero**

la po__ __ __ __ __ 'poverty'

la no__ __ __ __ __ 'nobility'

la li__ __ __ __ __ 'liberty, freedom'

17 From **ricco** and **forte**

la ri__ __ __ __ __ __ __ 'wealth'

la fo__ __ __ __ 'strength'

18 From **perdere** 'to lose'

per__ __ __ __ __ 'losing' (adj.), 'loser'

la per__ __ __ __ 'loss'

19 From **antico** 'ancient, antique'

l'anti__ __ __ __ __ 'antiquity'

l'anti__ __ __ __ __ __ __ 'antiques'

l'anti__ __ __ __ __ __ 'antique dealer'

20 From **servire** 'to serve'

il/la se__ __ __ /**-a** 'servant'

la ser__ __ __ __ 'servitude, servants'

__ __ __ __ __ **zie** __ __ __ __ 'helpful'

__ __ __ **vi** __ __ 'servile'

21 From **lo/-a schiavo/-a** slave

la __ __ __ __ __ __ __ __ __ 'slavery'

22 From **l'eroe** 'hero'

l'ero__ __ __ 'heroine, heroin'

l'ero__ __ __ __ 'heroism'

ero__ __ __ 'heroic'

23 From **la rivoluzione** 'revolution'

il/la ri_ _ _ _ _ _ _ _ _ _ _ _ _ _ _/-a 'revolutionary'

_ _ _ _ _ _ _rivo_ _ _ _ _ _ _ _ _ _ _/-a
'counter-revolutionary'

24 From **la lotta** 'fight, struggle, wrestling'

lo_ _ _ _ _ _ **con** 'to struggle, fight'

la _ _ _ _ _ _ **di** _ _ _ _ _ _ _ 'class struggle'

25 From **la ribellione** 'rebellion'

ri_ _ _ _ _ _ _ _ _   _ _ _ _ _ _ _ 'to rebel against'

ri_ _ _ _ _ _ 'rebellious'

il/la ri_ _ _ _ _ _ 'rebel'

26 From **la tregua** 'truce'

_ _ _ _ _ _ **tregua** 'relentless(ly)'

27 From **la pace** 'peace'

rappa_ _ _ _ _ _ _ _ _ 'to reconcile'

pa_ _ _ _ _ _ _ _ 'pacific'

il/la pa_ _ _ _ _ _ _ _ 'pacifist'

28 From **la storia** 'history, story'

_ _ _ _ _ _ _ _ 'historic, historical'

lo/-a_ _ _ _ _ _ _ _ _/-a 'historian'

Finally, complete the following list of '-isms':

29 'militarism'   _ _ _ _ _ _ _ _ _ _ _ _

'patriotism'   _ _ _ _ _ _ _ _ _ _ _

'nationalism'   _ _ _ _ _ _ _ _ _ _ _

'communism'   _ _ _ _ _ _ _ _ _

30 'fascism'   _ _ _ _ _ _ _ _

'colonialism'   _ _ _ _ _ _ _ _ _ _ _ _

'expansionism'   _ _ _ _ _ _ _ _ _ _ _ _ _

'pacifism'   _ _ _ _ _ _ _ _ _

See for further information
Soluzioni!, pages 17, 184
A Reference Grammar of Modern Italian, Chapter 21

Key points:
Using the imperfect correctly

*Do you find the imperfect confusing and difficult to use? Are you often in doubt whether to express an action with the imperfect or with the **passato prossimo**? This chapter will try and simplify the notion of the imperfect, with a view to making decisions on tenses easier and more straightforward.*

I   Describing past actions: what was happening?

One of the main uses of the imperfect is as a *descriptive* tense. This means essentially that what is important is not what *happened* but what *was happening*, not what the subject *did* but what s/he/it *was doing*. To stress this notion you can in English use a continuous tense (e.g. 'I was reading'), which will suggest you need an imperfect in Italian. If you are unsure whether a past action is descriptive, try asking yourself whether the action is telling us what *was happening* rather than what *happened*, or try replacing the English past tense with a continuous tense. If either (or both) of these work, you need an imperfect in Italian. Here are some examples:

> **La gente camminava svelta perché pioveva.**
> [The people walked (were walking) quickly because it was raining.]
> **Paolo studiava in camera sua, preparava gli esami.**
> [Paolo worked (was working) in his room, he prepared (was preparing) for his exams.]
> **La doccia non funzionava, i letti scricchiolavano e le finestre non si chiudevano bene: che camera!**
> [The shower didn't work (wasn't working), the beds creaked (were creaking) and the windows didn't shut (weren't shutting) properly: what a room!]

If the sentence contains a notion of how long the action lasted (e.g. 'for two hours', 'in five minutes', 'from 5 till 6', 'all day'), this suggests that *what happened* is more important. In these cases you should use the **passato prossimo**. Here are some examples:

> **Abbiamo camminato tutto il pomeriggio.**
> [We walked all afternoon.]
> **È piovuto dalle due alle sette.**
> [It rained from two till seven.]

Paolo ha studiato in camera sua per tre ore.
[Paolo worked in his room for three hours.]
Paolo ha preparato gli esami in sei settimane.
[Paolo prepared for his exams in six weeks.]

Complete the following sentences with the correct tense of the verb(s) in brackets:

---

1 All'incrocio, il vigile .... (dirigere) il traffico.
At the crossroads, the traffic policeman directed the traffic flow.

2 Il bambino .... (piangere) nel suo lettino.
The baby cried in his cot.

3 - **4** Il bambino .... (cadere) e .... (piangere) per dieci minuti.
The baby fell and cried for ten minutes.

5 In quel negozio ieri .... (vendere) dei bellissimi oggetti di ceramica.
They were selling some very pretty pottery in that shop yesterday.

6 Finalmente Giulia mi .... (vendere) uno dei suoi quadri.
Giulia has at last sold me one of her pictures.

7 - **8** Riccardo .... (suonare) il suo pezzo preferito al pianoforte e tutti
.... (ascoltare) senza fiatare.
Richard was playing his favourite piece on the piano and everybody was listening to him without saying a word.

9 Durante il concerto, il pianista .... (suonare) tre pezzi di Mozart.
During the concert, the pianist played three pieces by Mozart.

II Describing situations: what was it like?

Another very important use of the imperfect is to describe a situation, i.e. to say what things or people were like in the past. So, verbs stating:

- physical, psychological or emotional characteristics of people
- health and age
- physical characteristics of things and places
- time, dates and seasons
- the weather
- states of being

will all require the imperfect, unless there is a specific indication of the duration of the situation or state. Look at the following examples:

Massimo era un bambino piccolo e magro; aveva i capelli corti e biondi e portava gli occhiali. Spesso metteva i vestiti del fratello maggiore che non gli andavano bene. Era un bambino dolce, ma triste. Spesso stava male, aveva o la

febbre o il raffreddore e la tosse. Era sempre indaffarato, non aveva mai tempo di fermarsi a parlare. Viveva nel suo mondo.

[Massimo was a small, thin child; he had short blond hair and wore glasses. He often wore his elder brother's clothes, which did not fit him. He was a sweet child, but sad. He was often poorly, he had either a temperature or a cold and a cough. He was always busy, never had time to stop and talk. He lived in his own world.]

Era tardi, erano già le undici e anche se era estate, faceva fresco.

[It was late, it was eleven already and although it was summer, it was cool.]

La città era deserta e calda: tutti erano in vacanza.

[The city was deserted and hot: everyone was on holiday.]

Ho portato gli occhiali per molti anni, prima di mettere le lenti a contatto.

[I wore glasses for many years, before wearing contact lenses.]

La settimana scorsa sono stato male, ho avuto la febbre per tre giorni.

[Last week I was ill, I had a temperature for three days.]

L'estate scorsa è stata particolarmente calda.

[Last summer was particularly hot.]

Complete the following sentences with the correct tense of the verb(s) in brackets:

10 - 11 Suo padre non .... (essere) vecchio, ma .... (avere) l'aria stanca.
His father was not old, but he looked tired.

12 Marco .... (avere) l'ulcera per molti anni, ma adesso sta bene.
Mark had a stomach ulcer for many years, but now he's fine.

13 - 14 Non .... (avere) nessun interesse, ... (essere) molto pigri.
They had no interests, they were very lazy.

15 - 16 Che ora .... (essere) quando .... (arrivare), ragazzi?
What time was it when you arrived, boys?

17 .... (essere) due ore dal dentista!
We were at the dentist's for two hours!

18 Marina .... (avere) sempre i capelli lunghi.
Marina has always had long hair.

19 - 20 Marina .... (essere) molto carina: .... la frangia e le lentiggini.
Marina was very pretty: she had a fringe and freckles.

III   Habitual actions in past: what used to happen

The third major area of use of the imperfect is to indicate a habitual past action, i.e. what people used to do or what things used to be like. These are fairly easy to identify, as they are often expressed by 'used to' or 'would' in English. Here are some examples:

Qualche anno fa uscivamo spesso insieme.
[Some years ago we would often go out together.]
Quando abitavano in Italia, andavano a sciare sulle Dolomiti.
[When they lived in Italy, they used to go skiing in the Dolomites.]
Da bambino, non mangiava mai la verdura.
[As a child, he would never eat vegetables.]

IV   Other notable features of the imperfect

You have already come across the construction with **da** and the imperfect in Day 7, to mean that the subject *had been doing* something *for* or *since* a specific time.

With some verbs, it is important to know the difference in meaning between their imperfect and **passato prossimo** forms, as this will make things much easier when it comes to choosing the correct form. Look at the following list:

sapevo I knew (things, how to)	**ho saputo** I found out, I heard
conoscevo I knew (people, places)	**ho conosciuto** I met
pensavo di I was considering	**ho pensato di** I have decided to
dovevo I was supposed to	**ho dovuto** I've had to
volevo I meant to, I intended to	**ho voluto** I've wanted to
potevo I could	**ho potuto** I've been able to

As ever, the imperfect indicates a situation or condition, while the **passato prossimo** states that the action actually took (or didn't take) place. Here are some examples:

Non sapevo che Piero abitasse in centro.
[I didn't know that Piero lived in the town centre.]
Sapevi che Giuliana si sposa? – Sì, lo sapevo. L'ho saputo dalla sorella di Giuliana.
[Did you know that Giuliana is getting married? – Yes, I did. I heard it from Giuliana's sister.]
Vi conoscevate? – Sì, ci siamo conosciuti alla festa di Stefania.
[Did you know each other? – Yes, we met at Stefania's party.]

Pensavo di fare una torta, che ne dici?
[I was thinking about/considering making a cake. How about it?]
Claudia ha pensato di non iscriversi al corso di salsa.
[Claudia has decided not to enrol in the salsa class.]
Dovevamo andare in banca, ma abbiamo fatto tardi.
[We were supposed to go to the bank, but we were too late.]
Hai dovuto cambiare altri soldi?
[Have you had to change more money?]
Silvia voleva comprare il vestito rosso, ma non c'era la sua taglia.
[Silvia wanted to/meant to buy the red dress, but they didn't have her size.]

Complete the following sentences with the correct tense of the verb(s) in brackets:

---

21 .... (dire) sempre la verità quando ero piccola.
I would always tell the truth when I was little.

22 Mia madre mi .... (dire) sempre di non fidarmi dei commercianti.
My mother has always told me not to trust shopkeepers.

23 Mamma, quando .... (conoscere) papà?
Mum, when did you meet Dad?

24 .... (sapere) che cerchi lavoro, è vero?
I've heard you are looking for a job, is it true?

25 .... (pensare) di mandare una cartolina a Roberto.
We were thinking about sending Roberto a postcard.

26 .... (pensare) di mandare una cartolina a Roberto.
We have decided to send Roberto a postcard.

Finally, change the following sentences from the present to the past:

---

27 - 28 Mentre guido, guardo per caso nello specchietto: dietro di me c'è una macchina nera che mi segue.
As I'm driving, I casually take a look in the rear view mirror: behind me there is a black car which is following me.

....

....

---

29 – 30 **Una mia amica vuole una borsa di pelle per il suo compleanno, così giro tutti i**
negozi del centro per ore ma non riesco a trovare la borsa che vuole lei.
A friend of mine wants a leather handbag for her birthday,
so I go round all the city centre shops for hours, but I can't find
the bag she wants.

....

....

See for further information
Soluzioni!, pages 215–218
A Reference Grammar of Modern Italian, Chapter 15.12

Geographical vocabulary is useful for narrative purposes and for non-fictional contexts. Accuracy in this area will greatly improve your spoken and written Italian, and the odd specialized or unusual word will add style and sophistication.

la carta geografica/la cartina map
la carta politica political map, political landscape
il mappamondo globe, map of the world

la catena montuosa mountain range
le Alpi Alps
alpino alpine
l'alpinismo mountain climbing
gli Appennini Appennines
appenninico Appennine (adj.)
la catena chain
incatenare to chain

ai piedi di at the foothills of

la valle valley
valligiano valley dweller

la montagna mountain
in montagna in/to the mountains
montano mountain (adj.)
il montanaro mountain dweller

la collina hill
in collina on/to the hills
collinare hill (adj.)
collinoso hilly

la pianura plain
la Pianura Padana the Po Valley
pianeggiante flat, level

---

1 Guess the meaning of **la catena alimentare:**
....

2 Guess 'chain reaction':
la _ _ _ _ _ _ _ _ a _ _ _ _ _ _ _

3 Guess the meaning of **il clima montano:**
....

il nord north	**il sud** south
a nord in/to the north	**a sud** in/to the south
verso nord northwards	**verso sud** southwards
del nord northern	**del sud** southern
nordico nordic	**australe** of the southern hemisphere
il settentrione north	**il meridione/il mezzogiorno** south
settentrionale northern, northerner	**meridionale** southern, southerner
il nord-est north-east	**il sud-est** south-east
il nord-ovest north-west	**il sud-ovest** south-west
l'est (m.)/**l'oriente** (m.)/**il Levante** east	**l'ovest** (m.)/**l'occidente** (m.)/**il Ponente** west
ad est/in oriente/a Levante in/to the east	**ad ovest/in occidente/a Ponente** in/to the west
verso est/oriente/levante eastwards	**verso ovest/occidente/ponente** westwards
dell'est/orientale eastern	**dell'ovest/occidentale** western

---

4 Guess the meaning of **la crisi medio-orientale:**

....

5 Guess 'the Far Eastern countries':
i Paesi dell'Estremo __ __ __ __ __ __ __

6 Guess the meaning of **la terra del sol levante:**

....

---

la costa coast	**il mare** sea
costiero coastal	**al mare** at/to the seaside
il litorale coast(line)	**un mare di** stacks of, piles of
litoraneo coastal	**marino** sea (adj.)
il lago lake	**la marea** tide
lacustre lake (adj.)	**una marea di gente** hordes of people
il fiume river	**la riva** shore, bank
a fiumi in torrents	

---

7 Guess the meaning of **promettere mare e monti:**

....

8 Guess 'on the seashore':
in __ __ __ __ **al** __ __ __ __

Now complete the following sentences with the missing words:

> **9** __ _____ dell'Inghilterra è la regione più ricca del Paese.
> *The south-east of England is the richest part of the country.*
>
> **10** È una ditta con succursali in quasi tutti i Paesi dell'Europa _____.
> *It is a company with branches in almost every Western European country.*
>
> **11** I popoli dell'Europa _____ hanno uno stile di vita invidiato dal resto del continente.
> *The southern Europeans have a lifestyle that is the envy of the rest of the continent.*
>
> **12** Parto domani per le vacanze ma ho ancora __ _____ __ lavoro da sbrigare.
> *I'm going on holiday tomorrow but I still have stacks of work to do.*

The following set is a small selection of proper nouns relating to geography. Remember that only place names have initial capitals in Italian; the adjectives and the nouns denoting the people from the place are not capitalized. The easiest and most common ones (such as **Francia–francese**) have not been included to leave space for the slightly trickier or less common ones. If you have an interest in a corner of the world that is not included in the list below, make sure you know the Italian for all the relevant place names and their adjectives, so that you can talk and write about it with confidence if the opportunity arises.

Parigi; **parigino** Paris; Parisian
Marsiglia; **marsigliese** Marseilles; person from Marseilles and French national anthem

Londra; **londinese** London; Londoner
Edimburgo Edinburgh
il Galles; **gallese** Wales; Welsh
il Principe di Galles Prince of Wales
la contea county
il conte count (title of nobility), earl
il ducato duchy
il duca duke

il Belgio; **belga** (m. and f. s.; the plurals are **belgi** and **belghe**) Belgium; Belgian

le Fiandre; **fiammingo** Flanders; Flemish

la Grecia; **greco** (the plurals are **greci** and **greche**) Greece; Greek
Atene Athens

i Paesi Bassi; **olandese** the Netherlands; Dutch
l'Aja the Hague

la Svezia; **svedese** Sweden; Swedish, Swede
la rapa svedese swede
Stoccolma Stockholm

la Danimarca; **danese** Denmark; Danish, Dane

la Polonia; **polacco** Poland; Polish, Pole
Varsavia Warsaw

il Marocco; **marocchino** Morocco; Moroccan
Tàngeri Tangier

la Romania; **rumeno** Rumania; Rumanian

il Libano; **libanese** Lebanon; Lebanese

la Germania; **tedesco** Germany; German
Mònaco Munich and Monaco

l'Austria; **austriaco** Austria, Austrian

la Gran Bretagna, **il Regno Unito**; **britannico** Great Britain, the UK;
British

la Spagna; **spagnolo** Spain; Spanish
Barcellona Barcelona

il Portogallo; **portoghese** Portugal; Portuguese

gli Stati Uniti; **statunitense** the USA, USA (adj.)

Venezia; **veneziano** Venice; Venetian

Firenze; **fiorentino** Florence; Florentine

Now complete the following sentences with the missing words:

13 Mair è di Cardiff. È _ _ _ _ _ _ _.
Mair is from Cardiff. She is Welsh.

14 La moda _ _ _ _ _ _ _ _ _ mi piace meno di quella milanese.
I prefer Milan to Paris fashion.

15 – **16** Sono nata a Venezia ma i miei sono di Firenze, allora non so se sentirmi

_ _ _ _ _ _ _ _ _ _ o _ _ _ _ _ _ _ _ _ _ _.

I was born in Venice but my parents are from Florence, so I don't know whether to feel Venetian or Florentine.

17 – **19** Nelle scuole italiane ci sono sempre più bambini _ _ _ _ _ _ _ _ _ _,

_ _ _ _ _ _ _ _ e _ _ _ _ _ _.

Increasingly in Italian schools there are Moroccan, Polish and Rumanian children.

20 – **21** Il governo _ _ _ _ _ _ _ _ _ _ e quello _ _ _ _ _ _ _ _ _ _ _ hanno rapporti di collaborazione molto stretti.

The UK and USA governments have very close links.

---

la statistica statistic(s) (The singular indicates the discipline, the plural a set of statistics.)
lo/la statistico/-a statistician
la cifra figure (number)

la percentuale percentage
aumentare/diminuire del 10% (dieci per cento) to go up/down by 10%

la media average

il paese village
paesano village (adj.), villager
il paesaggio scenery, landscape
il/la paesaggista landscape painter

il panorama view, overview

la metropoli metropolis
la metropolitana underground

la piantina street plan
il piano plan (strategy), as in
il piano regolatore, town-planning scheme
pianificare to plan

l'edificio/la costruzione building
edificare/costruire to build
edile building (adj.), as in
  il cantiere edile building site
edificante edifying

il Paese/lo stato/la nazione country, state, nation
il/la connazionale fellow-countryman/woman

urbano urban
l'urbanesimo urbanization
l'urbanistica town planning

---

22 Guess the meaning of **la pianificazione familiare:**

....

23 Guess the meaning of **la leggenda metropolitana:**

....

24 Guess 'the developing countries':
i _ _ _ _ _ *in via di sviluppo*

25 Guess 'development plan':
il _ _ _ _ _ *di* _ _ _ _ _ _ _ _

---

il popolo people (Careful with agreement: the Italian word is singular.)
la popolazione population
popolare popular (i.e. people's), as in **il quartiere popolare** housing estate

l'emigrazione emigration	**l'immigrazione** immigration
emigrare emigrate	**immigrare** to immigrate
l'emigrato/-a emigré	**l'immigrato/-a** immigrant
	l'immigrato/-a economico/-a economic migrant
il/la profugo/-a refugee	**l'immigrato/-a clandestino/-a** illegal immigrant
l'extracomunitario/-a non-EU national/immigrant	

Now complete the following sentences with the missing words:

26 I bellissimi _ _ _ _ _ _ _ _ toscani hanno ispirato moltissimi poeti e artisti, sia italiani che stranieri.
The outstandingly beautiful Tuscan scenery has inspired very many poets and artists, both Italian and foreign.

27 Alla premiazione, l'orchestra ha suonato la _ _ _ _ _ _ _ _ _ _ _, l'inno nazionale francese.
At the prize-giving ceremony, the orchestra played the Marseillaise, the French national anthem.

28 – **29** Il vero problema non sono gli _ _ _ _ _ _ _ _ _ con regolare permesso di soggiorno, ma i _ _ _ _ _ _ _ _ _ _ _ _.
It is not the immigrants with a regular residence permit who are the real problem, but the illegal ones.

30 Le _ _ _ _ _ _ _ _ _ _ _ della disoccupazione giovanile in Italia dipingono un quadro molto più negativo di quello reale.
The statistics on young people's unemployment in Italy paint a much more negative picture than the real one.

Key points:
Verb constructions – the future of probability

The way in which verbs are constructed, i.e. whether they have a direct or indirect object and what preposition follows them, varies considerably between English and Italian. In order to avoid errors, it is important to know the correct construction of the main verbs and to check in your dictionary whenever you are not sure. This chapter will highlight the main differences in verb construction between English and Italian, to help you avoid those errors.

I Transitive/intransitive constructions

A transitive verb is one which can take a direct object, an intransitive verb one which cannot. Some Italian verbs, however, can be used both transitively and intransitively, depending on whether there is a subject doing the action or not. The distinction is very important in the **passato prossimo**, where the auxiliary being used depends on whether the verb is transitive (the auxiliary is **avere**) or intransitive (the auxiliary is **essere**). Here is a list of these verbs and some examples of their transitive and intransitive uses:

aumentare to increase	**finire** to finish
bruciare to burn	**iniziare** to begin
cambiare to change	**migliorare** to improve
cominciare to begin	**passare** to pass, spend time
cessare to cease	**peggiorare** to get worse
diminuire to decrease	**terminare** to end
continuare to continue	

> **I miei genitori mi hanno aumentato la paghetta settimanale.**
> [My parents have increased my weekly pocket money.]
> **I prezzi delle case sono aumentati ancora una volta.**
> [House prices have increased once again.]
> **Luciana ha cambiato tutti i mobili del salotto.**
> [Luciana has changed all her sitting-room furniture.]

Da quando frequenta l'università, Massimo è cambiato molto.
[Since he's been attending university, Massimo has changed a lot.]
Hai già cominciato a preparare la cena?
[Have you already begun to cook the dinner?]
Vieni a sederti, il tuo programma preferito è già cominciato!
[Come and sit down, your favourite programme has begun already!]
Grazie dell'invito, abbiamo passato una bella serata.
[Thank you for inviting us, we have spent a lovely evening.]
Quest'anno le vacanze sono passate in un baleno.
[This year the holidays have passed by in a flash.]

With some other verbs, the transitive construction has a different meaning from the intransitive one. Here are a list and some examples:

crescere to bring up (trans.), to grow (intrans.)
guarire to cure, to get better
importare to import, to matter
invecchiare to age, to grow old
ripassare to revise, to pass by again

saltare to skip, to jump
scattare to take a snapshot, to spring up
servire to serve, to need
toccare to touch, to have to

Hai ripassato matematica, Lorenzo?
[Have you revised your maths, Lorenzo?]
Non siamo più ripassati davanti a quel ristorante.
[We did not pass by that restaurant any more.]
Oggi ho saltato il pranzo, ho avuto troppo da fare.
[I skipped lunch today, I've had too much to do.]
Il gatto è saltato sul davanzale.
[The cat jumped onto the windowsill.]

In the following sentences, choose the correct auxiliary:

1   **Quando (ho/sono) iniziato a fare questo lavoro, eravamo solo in quattro.**
When I started doing this job, there were only four of us.

2   **La partita (ha/è) iniziata con cinque minuti di ritardo.**
The match started five minutes late.

3   **Il teatro (ha/è) bruciato completamente.**
The theatre burnt out completely.

4   **Mamma, corri, papà (ha/è) bruciato la cena!**
Mum, run, Dad's burnt the dinner!

5 **(Hanno/Sono) continuato a lavorare fino alle sei.**
They continued to work until six.

6 **Il rumore (ha/è) continuato per parecchie ore.**
The noise continued for several hours.

7 **Con questa pomata, la ferita (ha/è) guarita rapidamente.**
With this cream, the wound healed quickly.

8 **(Abbiamo/Siamo) servito il pranzo in terrazzo.**
We served lunch on the terrace.

9 **Alla fine i tuoi appunti non mi (hanno/sono) serviti.**
I did not need your notes in the end.

10 - **11** **Il pomeriggio (ha/è) passato e non (abbiamo/siamo) ancora cominciato a discutere il progetto.**
The afternoon has passed and we haven't yet begun to discuss the project.

II Verbs with different constructions in Italian

You should always beware of thinking in English and supposing that, because an English verb needs a preposition before a noun, the equivalent Italian verb will behave in the same way. The following four lists of verbs highlight the main differences:

- **verbs with direct object in Italian and with preposition in English**

  ascoltare to listen to
  approvare (una decisione) to approve of (a decision)
  aspettare to wait for
  cercare to look for
  chiedere/domandare to ask for
  guardare to look at
  pagare to pay for
  sognare to dream of

- **verbs with the preposition *a* in Italian and with direct object in English**

  assistere a to attend (an event, a show)
  assomigliare a to look like
  convenire a to suit
  giocare a to play
  disobbedire a to disobey
  obbedire a to obey
  permettere a to allow

resistere a to resist
rinunciare a to give up
rispondere a to answer
sopravvivere a to survive
telefonare a to telephone
voler bene a to love

- **verbs with the preposition *di* in Italian and with direct object in English**

  accorgersi di to notice
  aver bisogno di to need
  aver intenzione di to want
  aver voglia di to feel like
  dimenticarsi di to forget
  dubitare di to doubt
  fidarsi di to trust
  rendersi conto di to realize
  ricordarsi di to remember

- **verbs with different prepositions in Italian and English**

  congratularsi con to congratulate
  dare su to look out onto
  dipendere da to depend on
  finire per to end up
  lamentarsi di to complain about
  incidere su to affect
  preoccuparsi per to worry about
  ridere di to laugh about
  vivere di to live on

Once you have learnt these verbs, complete the following sentences with the correct preposition or leave blank if no preposition is required:

---

12 *Ogni mattina aspettiamo .... l'autobus alla stessa fermata.*
Every morning we wait for the bus at the same stop.

13 *Ho cercato .... quei documenti ma non li ho trovati.*
I looked for those documents but I did not find them.

14 *Che cosa hai risposto .... Maurizio?*
What did you answer Maurizio?

15 *Guardavano .... le nostre fotografie.*
They were looking at our photographs.

16 **Non abbiamo ancora telefonato .... Federica.**
We haven't 'phoned Federica yet.

17 **Laura non permette .... suoi bambini di andare a dormire tardi.**
Laura does not allow her children to go to bed late.

18 **Sai giocare .... scacchi?**
Can you play chess?

19 **Ci siamo congratulati .... Pietro per la sua laurea.**
We congratulated Pietro on his degree.

20 **Perché ridi ...... questa situazione?**
Why do you laugh about this situation?

21 **Ancora una volta hai disobbedito .... ai tuoi genitori.**
Once again you have disobeyed your parents.

22 **Purtroppo questa decisione non dipende ...... me.**
Unfortunately this decision does not depend on me.

III   The future of probability

The future tense is very often used in Italian to indicate speculation and probability. In this particular use, the simple future refers to speculation or probability related to the present, and the future perfect to speculation or probability related to the past. Look at the following examples:

> **Che ore saranno? – Non lo so, saranno le due.**
> [What time can it be? I don't know, it's probably two o'clock.]
> **Dove andrà Paola tutta in ghingheri?**
> [Where can Paola be going all dolled up?]
> **Giacomo non arriva ancora, che cosa sarà successo?**
> [Giacomo is not here yet, what can have happened?]

Now speculate on the possible reasons for a situation by using the future:

Marina piange, sai perché?

23 **......................... (ricevere) una brutta notizia.**
Maybe she's had some bad news.

24 **......................... (essere) giù.**
Maybe she's feeling down.

25 **......................... (litigare) di nuovo con il suo ragazzo.**
Maybe she's had another argument with her boyfriend.

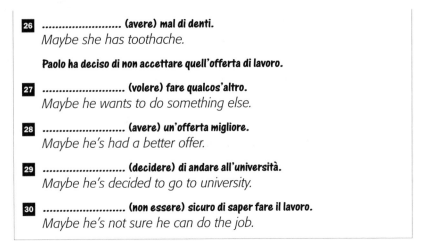

26 .... (avere) mal di denti.
Maybe she has toothache.

Paolo ha deciso di non accettare quell'offerta di lavoro.

27 .... (volere) fare qualcos'altro.
Maybe he wants to do something else.

28 .... (avere) un'offerta migliore.
Maybe he's had a better offer.

29 .... (decidere) di andare all'università.
Maybe he's decided to go to university.

30 .... (non essere) sicuro di saper fare il lavoro.
Maybe he's not sure he can do the job.

See for further information
Soluzioni!, Chapters 19 and 26
A Reference Grammar of Modern Italian, Chapters 15.5 and 17

Upgrade your style: Using the subjunctive

Most students shudder at the mere mention of the subjunctive, and it is true that some aspects of its use in Italian are very subtle and tricky to master. However, there are plenty of subjunctive constructions that are easy to use, and if you get into the habit of using them both in your written and in your spoken Italian, your style will significantly improve. The constructions discussed in this chapter all require the subjunctive: this means you don't have to decide between indicative and subjunctive, which is usually the trickiest part.

I Common verbs requiring the subjunctive

Out of all the verbs that require the subjunctive, **credere**, **pensare**, **sperare** and **temere** are the ones used most frequently. Provided it has a different subject, the following verb will always need to be in the subjunctive. Here are some examples:

> **Credo che la libertà di espressione sia un diritto fondamentale.**
> [I believe that freedom of expression is a fundamental right.]
> **Pensate che gli adolescenti guardino troppo la televisione?**
> [Do you think that teenagers watch too much television?]
> **Spero che la festa vi sia piaciuta.**
> [I hope you liked the party.]
> **Temo che sia troppo tardi per iscriversi.**
> [I am afraid it's too late to enrol.]

Additionally, the following frequently used verbal expressions will also require a subjunctive. Learn them and try to include them in your active vocabulary.

Speriamo che + present or past subjunctive, to express hope, as in:

> **Speriamo che il treno arrivi presto.**
> [Let's hope the train arrives soon.]
> **Speriamo che Giorgio non abbia già telefonato.**
> [Let's hope Giorgio hasn't already phoned.]

Mettiamo che + present or past subjunctive, to express supposition, as in:

> **Mettiamo che domani Paola non voglia venire con noi.**
> [Let's suppose that Paola does not want to come with us tomorrow.]
> **Mettiamo che questa lettera sia stata veramente scritta da lui.**
> [Let's suppose that this letter has really been written by him.]

Non vedo l'ora che + present subjunctive, to express longing, as in:

> **Non vedo l'ora che arrivi il fine-settimana!**
> [I can't wait for the weekend to arrive!]

Può darsi che + present or past subjunctive (the imperfect and pluperfect are also possible, for descriptive or imperfect actions in the past), to express probability, as in:

> **Può darsi che la biblioteca sia ancora aperta.**
> [Perhaps the library is still open.]
> **Può darsi che mio padre sia già tornato.**
> [Maybe my father has already returned.]
> **Può darsi che la ragazza con cui parlava fosse sua sorella.**
> [Maybe the girl he was talking to was his sister.]

Non è detto che + present or past subjunctive (the imperfect and pluperfect are also possible, for descriptive or imperfect actions in the past), to express doubt, as in:

> **Non è detto che la corruzione sia endemica.**
> [It's not definite that corruption is endemic.]
> **Non è detto che abbiano già cominciato.**
> [They won't necessarily have started already.]
> **Non è detto che fosse la soluzione migliore.**
> [It wasn't necessarily the best solution.]

Complete the following sentences using a verbal expression with the subjunctive:

1 .... che non .... troppo tardi.
Let's hope it's not too late.

2 .... davvero che lei .... ragione?
Do you really believe that she is right?

3 .... che il nostro problema maggiore .... la mancanza di fondi.
Our biggest problem isn't necessarily our lack of funds.

4 .... che .... le vacanze!
I can't wait for the holidays to start!

5 .... che la tua spiegazione .... poco convincente.
I am afraid that your explanation is not very convincing.

6 .... che .... la decisione più sensata.
I think they have taken the most sensible decision.

7 .... che ci .... due possibilità di interpretazione.
There may be two possible interpretations.

8 .... che lei .... già .... la verità.
Let's suppose she has already discovered the truth.

9 .... che la lettera non ....
Maybe the letter has not arrived.

10 .... che tutti .... d'accordo con te.
Not everybody necessarily agrees with you.

II Impersonal expressions requiring the subjunctive

Some impersonal verbs and many impersonal constructions with nouns or adjectives always require the subjunctive in a subordinate clause. They are used surprisingly frequently and can be very useful to 'spice up' your prose. Here are some examples:

Bisogna che + present subjunctive
Bisognava che + imperfect subjunctive, to express necessity, as in:

> **Bisogna che mi spieghiate chiaramente la situazione.**
> [You need to explain the situation clearly to me.]
> **Bisognava che parlassimo con il direttore.**
> [We needed to talk to the manager.]

È + adjective + **che** + present or past subjunctive
Era + adjective + **che** + imperfect or pluperfect subjunctive, as in:

> **È probabile che siano già partiti.**
> [It's likely that they have already left./They are likely to have already left.]
> **È normale che i giovani bevano così tanto?**
> [Is it normal for young people to drink so much?]
> **Era strano che litigassero.**
> [It was strange that they should argue.]
> **È meglio che finiate di studiare.**
> [It's better that you finish studying.]

È + noun + **che** + present or past subjunctive
Era + noun + **che** + imperfect or pluperfect subjunctive, as in:

> **È un peccato che dobbiate già andarvene.**
> [It's a pity that you must go already.]
> **È una vergogna/un'assurdità/una crudeltà che non ci sia acqua per tutti.**
> [It's a shame/an absurdity/a cruelty that there isn't water for all.]
> **Era una fortuna/una benedizione che ci fossero ancora persone così generose.**
> [It was lucky/a blessing that there should still be such generous people.]

È ora che + present subjunctive
Era ora che + imperfect subjunctive, 'It is/was time …', when the subordinate clause does not refer to the speaker, as in:

> **È ora che cessino le ostilità.**
> [It's time hostilities ceased.]
> **È ora che la smettiate di discutere.**
> [It's time you stopped arguing.]
> **Era ora che facessero qualcosa di concreto!**
> [It was high time they did something tangible!]

Complete the following sentences using an impersonal expression with the subjunctive:

11 .... che gli anziani .... (trattare) in questo modo.
It is a shame that the elderly are treated in this way.

12 ...... giusto che i dipendenti .... (fare) sciopero.
It is right that the employees should go on strike.

13 .... che la piscina .... aperta.
It was lucky that the swimming-pool was open.

14 .... che i giovani .... (volere) trasmissioni divertenti.
It's normal for young people to want amusing programmes.

15 .... prevedibile che gli uomini politici .... (dare) risposte evasive.
It was to be expected that politicians would give evasive answers.

16 .... che .... (sbrigarsi) se volete uscire.
You need to hurry if you want to go out.

17 .... che .... (sbrigarsi) se volevate uscire.
You needed to hurry if you wanted to go out.

18 .... **essenziale che tu** .... **(finire) prima di domani.**
It is essential that you finish before tomorrow.

19 .... **importante che ogni opinione** .... **(venire) ascoltata.**
It is important that every opinion is listened to.

20 .... **che** .... **(decidere) che cosa volete fare.**
It is time you decided what you want to do.

21 .... **che quest'ufficio** .... **sempre chiuso.**
It is absurd that this office is always closed.

22 .... **incredibile che** .... **(vincere) tutti quei soldi.**
It's incredible that he has won all that money.

III   Idiomatic expressions with the subjunctive

Several idiomatic expressions require the subjunctive but are easy and effective to use. Learn and try to use the following:

per + adjective + **che** + present or imperfect subjunctive, as in:

> **Per ridicolo che possa sembrare ...**
> [As ridiculous as it may seem ...]
> **Per assurdo che sia/fosse ...**
> [However absurd it is/was ...]

se solo + imperfect or pluperfect subjunctive, as in:

> **Se solo tu me lo avessi detto prima.**
> [If only you had told me before.]
> **Se solo mi dessero retta più spesso.**
> [If only they listened to me more often.]
> **Se solo non ci fossero così tanti pericoli.**
> [If only there weren't so many dangers.]

come se + imperfect or pluperfect subjunctive, as in:

> **Rideva come se fosse felice.**
> [S/he laughed as if s/he was happy.]
> **Fa' pure come se fossi a casa tua.**
> [Do exactly as if you were at home./Make yourself at home.]

Finally, remember the following idiomatic expressions with the subjunctive:

che io sappia	as far as I know
sia come sia	be as it may
vada come vada	whatever happens, be what may
sia detto per inciso	incidentally

Complete the following sentences using a suitable expression:

23 .... che ti .... (potere) sembrare, la mia decisione è
definitiva.
As absurd as it may seem to you, my decision is final.

24 .... (accorgersi) in tempo, avrei agito
diversamente.
If only I had realised it in time, I would have done it differently.

25 Gli parlava .... il loro padre.
He spoke to them as if he were their father.

26 ...., non legge romanzi gialli.
As far as I know, s/he does not read thrillers.

27 È un grande scrittore e, ..., lo è anche sua moglie.
He is a great writer and, incidentally, so is his wife.

28 ...., io sono dalla tua parte.
Whatever happens, I'm on your side.

29 .... bello ...., è talmente egocentrico che non piace a nessuno.
As handsome as he may be, he's so self-centred that nobody likes him.

30 Tratta la mia casa .... la sua.
S/he treats my house as if it were her/his own.

See for further information
Soluzioni!, Chapter 24
A Reference Grammar of Modern Italian, Chapter 15

A passive sentence stresses the action being done rather than the person or thing doing it. Using a passive sentence is a good way to upgrade your written style. The following exercises will help you get your passive sentences right and improve your style by using more sophisticated types of passive constructions.

I   Basic passive sentences

In a passive sentence, the action is 'being done' to the subject, rather than being performed by the subject: **il testimone è stato interrogato** [the witness has been questioned]. The person or thing doing the action, the agent, is introduced by **da** [by]: **la macchina era guidata da una donna** [the car was driven by a woman]. Only transitive verbs, i.e. verbs that can have an object, can be made passive. Here are some examples of active and passive sentences. As you can see, passive sentences use **essere**, and the past participle agrees with the subject.

La mia segretaria apre la posta.
[My secretary opens the post.]
La posta è aperta dalla mia segretaria.
[The post is opened by my secretary.]
La polizia raccoglierà le dichiarazioni dei testimoni.
[The police will collect the witnesses' statements.]
Le dichiarazioni dei testimoni saranno raccolte dalla polizia.
[The witnesses' statements will be collected by the police.]
I manifestanti hanno presentato una petizione.
[The demonstrators have presented a petition.]
Una petizione è stata presentata dai manifestanti.
[A petition has been presented by the demonstrators.]

What is the active form of **La macchina era guidata da una donna?**

1 ....

To help you, look at the following table:

Simple tenses	Passive form	Compound tenses	Passive form
guido	sono guidato	ho guidato	sono stato guidato
guiderò	sarò guidato	avrò guidato	sarò stato guidato
guidavo	ero guidato	avevo guidato	ero stato guidato
guidai	fui guidato		
guidi	sia guidato	abbia guidato	sia stato guidato
guidassi	fossi guidato	avessi guidato	fossi stato guidato
guiderei	sarei guidato	avrei guidato	sarei stato guidato
guidando	essendo guidato	avendo guidato	essendo stato guidato
guidare	essere guidato	aver guidato	essere stato guidato

Using the table as a guide, complete the following series of passive and active sentences:

2 **L'ingorgo è stato provocato da un incidente stradale.**
The traffic jam has been caused by a road accident.
Un incidente stradale .... l'ingorgo.
A road accident caused the traffic jam.

3 **Pare che molti danni all'agricoltura .... dai temporali estivi.**
It seems that much damage to agriculture is caused by summer storms.
Pare che i temporali estivi causino molti danni all'agricoltura.
It seems that summer storms cause much damage to agriculture.

4 **I nuovi contratti ....**
The new contracts will be refused by all.
Tutti rifiuteranno i nuovi contratti.

5 **La nostra doccia ....**
Our shower has not yet been repaired by the plumber.
Il nostro idraulico non ha ancora riparato la doccia.

6 **La spesa ....**
The shopping had already been done by the boys.
I ragazzi avevano già fatto la spesa.

7 **Sembra che l'auto ....**
It appears that the car was driven by a woman.
Sembra che una donna guidasse l'auto.

---

8 *Secondo i testimoni ....*
According to the witnesses, the car was driven by a woman.
Secondo i testimoni, una donna avrebbe guidato l'auto.

II Using *venire* in passive sentences

In simple tenses only, the verb **venire** can be used instead of **essere**. This stresses the action and looks very stylish. Here are some examples:

La posta è consegnata ogni giorno prima delle 9.
La posta viene consegnata ogni giorno prima delle 9.
[The post gets delivered every day before 9.]
L'assegno sarà addebitato domani.
L'assegno verrà addebitato domani.
[The cheque will be debited tomorrow.]
I programmi erano presentati da un'annunciatrice.
I programmi venivano presentati da un'annunciatrice.
[The programmes were introduced by an announcer.]
Pensavo che tutti fossero promossi, prima o poi.
Pensavo che tutti venissero promossi, prima o poi.
[I thought everybody got promoted, sooner or later.]

Try using it in the following sentences, to replace **essere**:

---

9 Assicuratevi che le scarpe sporche di fango non siano lasciate sul pavimento.
Make sure that muddy shoes are not left on the floor.

....

10 Molto spesso i pasti sono consumati davanti alla televisione.
Meals are very often eaten in front of the television.

....

11 Le auto erano sempre parcheggiate in doppia fila.
Cars were always double parked.

....

12 La spiegazione sarà ripetuta domani.
The explanation will be repeated tomorrow.

....

III Using *andare* and *rimanere* in passive sentences

In simple tenses only, the verb **andare** can be used in passive sentences to replace **dover essere** ('must be'), i.e. to express need or obligation. Like **essere** and **venire**, it is followed by the past participle. This is another very stylish construction, and not at all difficult to use. Look at the following examples:

> **La cartuccia della stampante è esaurita: va sostituita.**
> **La cartuccia della stampante è esaurita: deve essere sostituita.**
> [The printer cartridge is empty: it must be replaced.]
> **Le tende del salotto andrebbero lavate a secco.**
> **Le tende del salotto dovrebbero essere lavate a secco.**
> [The sitting room curtains should be dry-cleaned.]
> **La torta andava lasciata in forno almeno un altro quarto d'ora.**
> **La torta doveva essere lasciata in forno almeno un altro quarto d'ora.**
> [The cake should have been left in the oven another quarter of an hour at least.]

Rewrite the following sentences using **andare** instead of **dover essere**:

---

13 Questi moduli devono essere compilati e consegnati entro domani.
These forms must be filled in and handed in by tomorrow.

....

14 Il tuo vestito dovrebbe essere accorciato un po'.
Your dress should be shortened a little.

....

15 La mia macchina dovrà essere revisionata ad aprile.
My car will have to be MOT'd in April.

....

16 Pensavo che queste lettere non dovessero essere spedite oggi.
I thought these letters shouldn't have been sent today.

....

17 Credo che questa decisione debba essere presa da tutti.
I think that this decision must be taken by everyone.

....

18 Le piante da appartamento non devono essere innaffiate troppo.
House plants must not be over-watered.

....

With some verbs, which indicate loss and similar meanings, **andare** is used to replace **essere**. This use is restricted to the third persons. The verbs most often used with this type of construction are: **perdere**, **rovinare**, **distruggere**, **sprecare**, **dimenticare**, **disperdere**, **smarrire**. Here are some examples:

> **Nell'incidente, la nostra auto è andata completamente distrutta.**
> **Nell'incidente, la nostra auto è stata completamente distrutta.**
> [Our car has been totally destroyed in the accident.]
> **Mangiate i panini, altrimenti andranno sprecati.**
> **Mangiate i panini, altrimenti saranno sprecati.**
> [Eat the sandwiches, otherwise they'll go to waste.]

Using the translation to help you, complete the following sentences with the correct form of **andare**:

> **19** **Nella confusione, la mia bella sciarpa .... persa.**
> *In the rush, my lovely scarf has been lost.*
>
> **20** **Mettiamo qui le chiavi, in modo che non .... dimenticate.**
> *Let's put the keys here, so that they are not left behind.*
>
> **21** **Ancora una volta i nostri sforzi .... sprecati.**
> *Once again our efforts have been wasted.*

With verbs like **ferire**, **sconvolgere**, **bloccare**, **intrappolare**, **sorprendere**, to stress the impact of the action on the subject, **rimanere** is often used instead of **essere**. This type of passive sentence is often used in journalistic language, as it is an elegant way of emphasizing the action. Look at the following examples:

> **Se non prendi la chiave, rimarrai chiusa fuori!**
> **Se non prendi la chiave, sarai chiusa fuori!**
> [If you don't take your key, you'll be locked out!]
> **La mia vicina di casa è rimasta bloccata nell'ascensore.**
> **La mia vicina di casa è stata bloccata nell'ascensore.**
> [My next-door neighbour got trapped in the lift.]
> **Sembra che parecchie persone siano rimaste ferite nell'incidente.**
> **Sembra che parecchie persone siano state ferite nell'incidente.**
> [It seems that several people have been wounded in the accident.]

Now, try using **rimanere** instead of **essere** in the following sentences:

---

22 | **I due sciatori sono stati sepolti da una valanga.**
The two skiers have been buried by an avalanche.

....

23 | **Sarete scioccati anche voi quando saprete quello che è successo.**
You'll be shocked too, when you hear what happened.

....

24 | **Invece di alzarsi in piedi, gli spettatori erano stati seduti.**
Instead of standing up, the audience had remained sitting.

....

IV   Avoiding a common pitfall

In English it is possible to have a passive sentence which has as its subject the indirect object of a corresponding active sentence. So, from the active sentence: 'The teacher has given John a book', two passive sentences can be formed: 'A book has been given to John by the teacher' and, more elegantly and more likely, 'John has been given a book by the teacher'. This construction is common in passive sentences with verbs like 'to tell', 'to advise', 'to promise', 'to offer', 'to teach', 'to grant', 'to sell', 'to award', 'to ask', 'to deny', 'to show', 'to force', etc. This construction is not possible in Italian. The best way to avoid errors is to make the sentence active, using a hypothetical **loro** as a subject, particularly if there is no direct object. Look at the following examples:

> John has been given a book = A book has been given to John = They have given John a book
> = **Hanno dato a John un libro/A John hanno dato un libro.**
> We are told to go out = They tell us to go out
> = **Ci dicono di uscire.**
> She has been awarded a prize = They have awarded her a prize
> = **Le hanno assegnato un premio.**

If there is a direct object it is of course possible to have a passive sentence like: **A John è stato dato un libro**, or **Le è stato assegnato un premio.**
  Here are some more examples:

> [My father has been advised to rest.]
> **Hanno consigliato a mio padre di riposare.**
> [I had been taught the rules of the game.]
> **Mi avevano insegnato le regole del gioco.**
> [He is given antibiotics all the time.]
> **Gli dànno antibiotici tutto il tempo.**

[Consumers have been told to return the faulty product.]

Hanno detto ai consumatori di restituire il prodotto difettoso.

È stato detto ai consumatori di restituire il prodotto difettoso.

Now, give a suitable Italian translation for the following passive sentences:

---

25 I have been shown the new flat. ('to show' = **far vedere**)

....

26 We had been asked to pay for the photocopies.

....

27 She has been told not to go out.

....

28 They are given too many presents. ('to give presents' = **fare regali**)

....

29 He was promised a promotion.

....

30 You were being sold a faulty car!

....

For a passive construction which uses **si** and the third person of the verb, see Section I of Day 21.

See for further information
Soluzioni!, Chapter 25
A Reference Grammar of Modern Italian, Chapter 14

Upgrade your style: Rhetorical signposts and logical connectors

Rhetorical signposts point the readers of a text in the right direction and guide them through it. Using them competently in Italian is a good way to upgrade your written style, as you give your text a better structure and you make it more persuasive, sophisticated and interesting to read.

I   Signposting and sequencing

Whether your text is written or presented orally, it is essential to signal to your audience the stages in your argument.

Learn the following expressions and try to include them in your active vocabulary.

OPENING
prima di tutto first of all
per cominciare to begin with
anzitutto/innanzitutto first and foremost
in primo luogo in the first place

in fin dei conti ultimately, in the end
in ultima analisi in the final analysis
in definitiva all in all
insomma in a nutshell

SEQUENCING
successivamente next
in secondo luogo secondly
inoltre additionally, furthermore
quindi then

GENERALIZING
in genere/in generale generally, as a rule
per lo più mostly, by and large
in linea di massima on the whole
sostanzialmente/in sostanza essentially
fondamentalmente/in fondo basically

ENDING
infine finally
in conclusione/per concludere to end with
tutto sommato all things considered, all in all

Fill the gaps in the following sentences using appropriate expressions from the list above:

1 Vorrei .... ringraziarvi di avermi invitata a parlare.
I would like first of all to thank you for having invited me to speak to you.

2 .... dobbiamo esaminare il modo in cui l'autore ha definito i suoi personaggi nel primo capitolo.
In the first place we must look at how the author has outlined his characters in the first chapter.

3 .... il nostro problema maggiore è la mancanza di immaginazione.
All in all, our biggest problem is our lack of imagination.

4 .... dobbiamo cercare quali altri fattori possano aver contribuito a creare tale squilibrio.
Secondly, we must look for other factors which might have contributed to such an imbalance.

5 La spiegazione del fenomeno è .... convincente.
The explanation of the phenomenon is on the whole convincing.

6 .... tocca ai cittadini decidere del loro futuro.
Ultimately, it's the citizens who must decide their future.

7 Ci sono .... due possibilità di interpretazione.
There are essentially two possible interpretations.

II   Linking ideas: alternatives to *e*

Sometimes using **e** on its own to link ideas can be rather weak. To reinforce it, you can use a strengthening word like **addirittura**, **persino** [even], **per di più** [what's more, moreover], or an expression like **peggio/meglio ancora** [worse/better still]. Here are some examples:

> **In questa città la vita è stressante e alienante.**
> [Life in this city is stressful and alienating.]
> **In questa città la vita è stressante e addirittura alienante.**
> **In questa città la vita è stressante e per di più alienante.**
> **In questa città la vita è stressante e, peggio ancora, alienante.**

Alternatively, you can use one of the following expressions:

> **allo stesso tempo**, e.g. **per motivi politici ed allo stesso tempo sociali**
> [for political and at the same time social reasons]
> **non solo ... ma anche**, e.g. **In questa città la vita è non solo stressante, ma anche alienante.**
> [Life in this city is not just stressful, but also alienating.]

sia ... che, e.g. **Andiamo in montagna sia d'inverno che d'estate.**
[We go to the mountains in both winter and summer.]
tanto ... quanto, e.g. **Queste regole sono tanto difficili da accettare quanto da giustificare.**
[These rules are as difficult to accept as they are to justify.]
come pure, e.g. **Questi provvedimenti riguardano i dipendenti come pure i lavoratori in proprio.**
[These measures concern employees as well as self-employed people.]
oltre che + adj./**oltre a** + inf. or noun, e.g. **Oltre che stressante/ Oltre ad essere stressante, la vita in questa città è alienante.**
[Besides being stressful, life in this city is alienating.]

Rewrite the following sentences, finding a suitable way either to reinforce or to replace the conjunction **e**:

---

8 **Questo problema tocca da vicino i giovani e gli anziani.**
This problem affects young and old.
....

9 **I dipendenti di questa ditta sono sfruttati e sottopagati.**
In this company the employees are exploited and underpaid.
....

10 **La piscina è aperta d'estate e d'inverno.**
The swimming-pool is open in summer and in winter.
....

11 **I giovani telespettatori vorrebbero trasmissioni divertenti e istruttive.**
Young viewers would like amusing and educational programmes.
....

12 **Gli uomini politici, di destra e di sinistra, hanno dato risposte evasive.**
Right-wing and left-wing politicians have given evasive answers.
....

III   Logical sequence: conclusion or consequence
When you want to express the conclusion or the consequence of an action or event, stressing its outcome, there are several possibilities in Italian equivalent to 'so' or 'therefore'. You have probably already come across **e così** [and

so] or **e allora** [and then]. To ring the changes, you can use one of the following alternatives:

perciò for this reason, therefore	**di conseguenza** consequently, as a result
quindi hence, therefore	**ecco perché** so (=that's why)
dunque thus, so	**tanto che** so much so that
per cui for this reason, so	**al punto che** to the extent that, so much so that
pertanto thus, so	**di/in modo che** so that
	in modo da + infinitive so as to, in such a way as to

The expressions on the left are pretty much interchangeable; the ones on the right are more specific.

Here are some examples:

> **Era troppo tardi per uscire, perciò siamo rimasti a casa.**
> [It was too late to go out, so we stayed at home.]
> **Il mio ombrello vecchio è rotto, per cui ne dovrò comprare un altro.**
> [My old umbrella is broken, therefore I shall have to buy a new one.]
> **La camera era davvero rumorosa, tanto che me ne sono fatta dare un'altra.**
> [The room was really noisy, so much so that I got them to give me another one.]
> **Purtroppo non saremo in Italia, di conseguenza non potremo andare al loro matrimonio.**
> [Unfortunately we won't be in Italy, consequently we won't be able to go to their wedding.]
> **Bisogna agire in modo da non compromettere la situazione.**
> [It is necessary to act so as not to compromise the situation.]
> **Mettiamo qui le chiavi, in modo che non vadano perse.**
> [Let's put the keys here, so that they don't get lost.]

Complete the following sentences using a suitable expression from the list above:

---

13 Erano davvero stufi della sua maleducazione, ... si sono lamentati con i genitori.
They were really fed up with his bad manners, so much so that they complained to his parents.

---

14 **Il tuo vestito da sposa è davvero bellissimo: .... tutti lo ammirano.**
Your wedding dress is really beautiful: that's why everybody admires it.

15 **La mia macchina dovrà essere revisionata ad aprile, ... non posso portarla all'estero.**
My car will have to be MOT'd in April, as a result I can't take it abroad.

16 **Le risorse naturali scarseggiano .... dobbiamo ridurre il consumo di combustibili fossili.**
Our natural resources are in short supply, therefore we must cut our consumption of fossil fuels.

17 **Imparare a suonare uno strumento non è facile, ... devi applicarti.**
Learning to play an instrument is not easy, so you must apply yourself.

18 **Dovete organizzarvi .... avere il tempo di visitare l'esposizione.**
You must organize yourselves so as to have the time to visit the exhibition.

IV   Logical sequence: reason or cause

To stress the cause or reason behind an action or event, there are several possibilities equivalent to 'because' or 'since', in addition to **perché**.

Unlike 'since' and 'because', **perché** can never begin a sentence, so in such cases an alternative is required. You can use one of the following:

siccome since	**in quanto** inasmuch as, in that, in
dato che given that	view of the fact that
visto che seeing that	
considerato che bearing in mind that	**per il fatto che** because
dal momento che as, since	**per il motivo che** because
	per la ragione che because

Here are some examples:

> **Siccome i negozi saranno chiusi domani, facciamo la spesa oggi.**
> [As the shops will be shut tomorrow, let's do our shopping today.]
> **Visto che ci siamo tutti, possiamo cominciare.**
> [Seeing that we are all here, we can begin.]
> **Gli inglesi vanno in vacanza all'estero per il fatto che sul tempo inglese non si può fare affidamento.**
> [The English go on holiday abroad because one cannot count on the English weather.]

Dato che è il tuo compleanno, andiamo a mangiar fuori!
[As it's your birthday, let's eat out!]
Dal momento che sei qui, ti spiego la faccenda.
[As you are here, I'll explain the matter to you.]
Non è venuta alla partita, in quanto temeva di annoiarsi.
[She did not come to the match in view of the fact that she was afraid she'd be bored.]

Using the translation as guidance, rewrite the following sentences with a suitable alternative to **perché**:

19 Non hai nulla da temere perché ti sei scusato.

....

Given that you have apologized, you have nothing to fear.

20 Propongo che ci fermiamo qui perché sono già le sei.

....

Seeing that it is already six o'clock, I suggest we stop now.

21 L'obesità è in aumento perché le abitudini alimentari degli adolescenti sono
fondamentalmente sbagliate.

....

Obesity is on the increase inasmuch as teenagers' eating habits are basically wrong.

22 Hanno fatto male a disfarsi della loro auto vecchia, perché non sono sicuri di
quando arriverà quella nuova.

....

They were wrong to get rid of their old car, bearing in mind that they are not sure when the new one will arrive.

23 L'autore ha ringraziato tutti i suoi collaboratori perché lo avevano aiutato.

....

Since they had helped him, the author thanked all the contributors.

V   Contrasting/opposing
There are also several alternatives to **ma**. Here is a list of the different possibilities:

però but, however	**tuttavia** nevertheless, however
mentre whereas	**piuttosto** rather
invece however, on the other hand	**in realtà** in actual fact, actually
eppure and yet	**anche se** although
	d'altra parte on the other hand

del resto but then, on the other hand

da un lato ... dall'altro on the one hand ... on the other

da una parte ... dall'altra on the one hand ... on the other

anzi on the contrary, not at all

bensì but rather

Now look at the following examples:

Luciana non sopporta Johnny Depp, eppure è un attore così bravo!
[Luciana cannot stand Johnny Depp, and yet he's such a good actor!]

Non possiamo dire che metà della frutta è da buttare. D'altra parte, però, non si può nemmeno affermare che il 98% è sicuro.
[We cannot say that half the fruit is fit to be thrown away. But, on the other hand, one cannot state either that 98% of it is safe.]

Noi siamo andati in macchina, mentre loro hanno preferito la metropolitana.
[We went by bus, whereas they preferred the underground.]

Sono molto arrabbiata con voi, tuttavia so benissimo che non è stata solo colpa vostra.
[I am very cross with you; however I know very well that it wasn't just your fault.]

Gli uomini parlavano fra di loro; le donne, invece, stavano zitte.
[The men talked to one another; the women, on the other hand, were silent.]

Il film è stato lunghissimo; del resto, nessuno si è annoiato.
[The film was extremely long; on the other hand, no one got bored.]

Da una parte mi dispiace rifiutare il loro invito, dall'altra non mi diverto mai con loro.
[On the one hand I regret refusing their invitation; on the other I never enjoy myself with them.]

Diceva di essere imprenditore. In realtà, era un semplice dipendente.
[He said he was an entrepreneur. In actual fact, he was a simple employee.]

Le nozze non si svolgeranno in chiesa, bensì con una cerimonia civile.
[The wedding will not take place in church, but rather at a civil ceremony.]

Now, try using an alternative to **ma** in the following sentences. Use the translation as a guide and make any other necessary changes:

---

24 **Mi aveva detto che l'avrei trovata in ufficio, ma non c'era.**

....

She told me I would find her in her office, yet she wasn't there.

25 **L'economia è in continua crescita, ma i prezzi continuano a salire.**

....

The economy is growing all the time, although prices continue to rise.

26 **Non è un tentativo di mediazione, ma una vera provocazione.**

....

It is not an attempt to mediate, rather a real act of provocation.

VI   Learning to be flexible

A good way to check one's progress when learning a foreign language is to practise different ways of expressing the same idea. This teaches us to be more flexible, and adds variety and sophistication to our language. For example, the following two pairs of sentences express the same idea in two different ways: the first one stresses a fact and its consequence, while the second one the effect and its cause.

La mia penna stilografica perde inchiostro, di conseguenza dovrò farla riparare.
[My fountain pen is leaking ink; as a result I'll have to get it repaired.]
Dovrò far riparare la mia penna stilografica, in quanto perde inchiostro.
[I'll have to get my fountain pen repaired, in view of the fact that it's leaking ink.]
Beatrice ha preso il sole per ore ogni giorno, tanto che si è scottata.
[Beatrice sunbathed for hours every day, so much so that she got sunburnt.]
Beatrice si è scottata, siccome ha preso il sole per ore ogni giorno.
[Beatrice got sunburnt because she sunbathed for hours every day.]

Now, give a suitable alternative for the following sentences, making any necessary change:

---

27 **Dal momento che non abbiamo molto tempo, faremmo meglio a sbrigarci.**
As we don't have much time, we had better hurry.

....

28 **Lorenzo soffriva di raffreddore da fieno, per cui non gli piaceva l'estate.**
Lorenzo suffered from hay fever, so he did not like the summer.

....

29 **Leggete Shakespeare a scuola per il fatto che è considerato un autore fondamentale.**
You read Shakespeare at school because he's considered an essential author.

....

30 **Non porteranno la carta di credito, pertanto dovranno pagare in contanti.**
They won't bring their credit card, so they'll have to pay in cash.

....

See for further information
Soluzioni!, Chapter 16
A Reference Grammar of Modern Italian, Chapter 19

Key points: Infinitive vs. gerund

Are you sometimes unsure how to put words ending in '-ing' into Italian? This chapter will look in detail at some of the most common sources of error when translating '-ing' forms.

I After verbs and prepositions

The '-ing' form is very often found after verbs, with or without a preposition, as in the following examples:

Would you mind moving your car?
We love dancing.
They went skiing last week.

He must do it without looking.
I am used to waiting.

Do you feel like eating now?
I really look forward to reading this book.
Before returning home, we should buy something to drink.

In all of these cases, in Italian you must use the infinitive, with or without a preposition:

Le dispiacerebbe spostare la macchina?
Ci piace moltissimo ballare.
Sono andati a sciare la settimana scorsa.

Deve farlo senza guardare.
Sono abituato ad aspettare.

Hai voglia di mangiare adesso?
Non vedo l'ora di leggere questo libro.
Prima di tornare a casa, dovremmo comprare qualcosa da bere.

The infinitive is also used after verbs of perception like **vedere** and **sentire** in sentences like:

L'ho visto uscire dalla banca un'ora fa.
[I saw him coming out of the bank an hour ago.]

In città non sentiamo più cantare gli uccelli.
[In the city, we don't hear the birds singing any more.]
È stato visto salire su una macchina grigia.
[He was seen getting into a grey car.]

Fill the gaps in the following sentences:

1 **Devi continuare ad .... se vuoi migliorare.**
You must keep on training if you want to improve.

2 **Ha saggiamente evitato di .... dell'incidente con il capo.**
He wisely avoided talking about the incident with his boss.

3 **L'hanno detto senza .... alle conseguenze.**
They said it without thinking of the consequences.

4 **Leggi il libro prima di .... a vedere il film.**
Read the book before going to see the film.

5 **Smettetela di .... tutto questo rumore!**
Stop making all this noise!

6 **Litigano sempre: li sentiamo .... da casa nostra.**
They are always arguing: we hear them shouting from our house.

7 **Cerca di evitare di .... nell'ora di punta.**
Try to avoid travelling in the rush hour.

8 **Non l'avevamo mai vista ....: è bravissima!**
We had never seen her dancing: she's really good!

II   'After' + '-ing' form

To translate expressions like 'after waiting', you must use the preposition **dopo** followed by the compound infinitive, i.e. the auxiliary **essere** or **avere** + the past participle of the verb. Any pronoun will be attached to the auxiliary:

Dopo aver parlato con Mauro, ho capito tutto.
[After speaking to Mauro, I understood everything.]
Si sono sposati dopo essere usciti insieme per sei mesi.
[They got married after going out together for six months.]
Dopo averti aspettato per due ore, sono tornato a casa.
[After waiting for you for two hours, I returned home.]
Dopo essersi laureati, cercheranno un lavoro.
[After graduating, they will look for a job.]

In one case only the auxiliary is not used: **dopo mangiato** [after eating].

Fill the gaps in the following sentences:

> **9** Dopo .... i compiti, sono usciti.
> *After finishing their homework, they went out.*
>
> **10** Dopo .... da cavallo, ha subito due operazioni.
> *After falling from her horse, she has undergone two operations.*
>
> **11** Me ne andrò solo dopo .... con il direttore.
> *I shall leave only after talking to the manager.*
>
> **12** Dopo .... in Giappone, vorrebbero andare in Cina.
> *After being in Japan, they would like to go to China.*

III   When the '-ing' form is a noun
Quite often the '-ing' form is used as a noun, in sentences like:

> Listening to music is a very common pastime.
> I find reading very useful to relax.
> Taking so many exams means no holidays for three years.

In this case, too, in Italian you must use the infinitive:

> **Ascoltare musica è un passatempo molto diffuso.**
> **Trovo che leggere sia molto utile per rilassarsi.**
> **Dare così tanti esami vuol dire niente vacanze per tre anni.**

Complete the following sentences:

> **13** .... fa molto bene a chi ha mal di schiena.
> *Swimming is very good for those who have backache.*
>
> **14** È una persona solitaria: .... a scacchi è il suo unico interesse.
> *He's a lonely person: playing chess is his only interest.*
>
> **15** Pensi che .... con la febbre sia una buona idea?
> *Do you think that going out with a temperature is a good idea?*

IV   'When' and 'while' + '-ing' form; '-ing' form + noun
Expressions like 'when speaking', 'while walking' are fairly common in English. One way to translate them into Italian is to 'open up' the expression (but see also Section V). For example:

> When travelling by train, I often read a book.

is the same as:

> When I am travelling by train, I often read a book.

> While watching TV, he managed to finish his homework.

is the same as:

> While he was watching TV, he managed to finish his homework.

So:

Quando viaggio in treno, leggo spesso un libro.
Mentre guardava la TV, è riuscito a finire i compiti.

In instances when the '-ing' form after a noun describes what that noun is doing (as in 'the people working on a project'), you MUST 'open up' the expression. For example:

> The company offering the best deal will win the contract

is the same as:

> The company which is offering the best deal will win the contract.

> The people following his advice could find themselves in trouble.

is the same as:

> The people who follow his advice could find themselves in trouble.

So:

La ditta che farà l'offerta migliore vincerà il contratto.
Le persone che seguono i suoi consigli potrebbero trovarsi nei guai.

Now, complete the following sentences:

---

16 **L'ho incontrata ieri .... in centro.**
I met her yesterday while walking in the centre.

17 **Alla fermata c'erano almeno dieci persone .... l'autobus.**
At the bus stop there were at least ten people waiting for the bus.

18 **............................. oggetti costosi, devi chiedere la garanzia.**
When buying expensive items, you must ask for a guarantee.

V   Joining two actions

You can also use the '-ing' form to join two actions performed by the same subject in the same sentence. These two actions can be happening at the same time, one after another, or one can be explaining the reason for the other. Here are some examples:

He walked away, whistling. (He walked away, he was whistling.)
They have arrived together, carrying a huge parcel. (They arrived, they were carrying a huge parcel.)
Realizing I could do nothing to help, I changed my mind. (I realized, I changed my mind.)
Being so athletic, Tom will be a good mountain climber. (Since/Because he is so athletic, he will be a good mountain climber.)

In all these cases, in Italian you need to use a gerund:

Se n'è andato fischiettando.
Sono arrivati insieme, portando un pacco enorme.
Rendendomi conto di non poter far nulla per aiutare, ho cambiato idea.
Essendo così atletico, Tom sarà un bravo alpinista.

If you want to stress the fact that one action happens before the other, use the compound gerund:

Essendomi reso conto di non poter far nulla, ho cambiato idea.
[Having realized I could do nothing, I changed my mind.]
Avendo letto fino a tardi ieri sera, ha dormito poco.
[Having read till late last night, he had little sleep.]

Complete the following sentences:

> **19** .... un po' sciocco, non ho detto nulla.
> *Feeling a little foolish, I said nothing.*
>
> **20** .... dei soldi dai suoi genitori, si è comprata un computer nuovo.
> *Having received some money from her parents, she has bought herself a new computer.*
>
> **21** Comprerà dei fiori per la nonna, ... che le piacciano.
> *He will buy some flowers for his Gran, hoping she will like them.*

The gerund is used with **pur** to mean 'despite', 'although', as in:

> **Pur essendo fratelli, non si sopportano.**
> [Despite being brothers, they can't stand each other.]
> **Pur avendolo letto parecchie volte, non sono sicuro di aver capito questo articolo.**
> [Although I have read/Despite having read it several times, I am not sure I have understood this article.]

Complete the following sentences:

> **22** .... bene, non so come si comporterebbe in questa situazione.
> *Despite knowing him well, I don't know how he would behave in this situation.*
>
> **23** .... a Roma da tre anni, non parlano italiano.
> *Although they have been living in Rome for three years, they don't speak Italian.*

The translation of sentences with 'when' and 'while' we saw in Section IV could also feature a gerund, as they describe two actions joined together. So:

viaggiando in treno

is the same as:

quando viaggio in treno.

Guardando la TV

is the same as:

mentre guardava la TV.

DAY 17: INFINITIVE VS. GERUND

Don't forget that the gerund is also used with **stare**, to stress that an action is taking place at a particular time:

> **Sto scrivendo alla mia corrispondente.**
> [I am writing to my penfriend.]
> **Quando siamo arrivati, stavano parlando con l'allenatore.**
> [When we arrived, they were talking to the trainer.]

VI   The '-ing' form as an adjective

Many English adjectives end in '-ing'. They describe a characteristic of a noun. For example:

> an amusing novel
> a surprising number of people
> a convincing example

In a lot of cases, the equivalent form in Italian is a present participle, used as an adjective. As in English, all of these are derived from verbs. Here is a list of common ones:

accogliente	welcoming	**pendente**	leaning
affascinante	charming	**perdente**	losing
bollente	boiling	**precedente**	preceding
cadente	falling	**rampicante**	climbing
commovente	moving	**rassicurante**	reassuring
convincente	convincing	**rinfrescante**	refreshing
corrente	running	**scrosciante**	pouring
divertente	amusing	**seccante**	annoying
entusiasmante	exciting	**seguente**	following
fiorente	flourishing	**soffocante**	suffocating
frizzante	sparkling	**sorprendente**	surprising
idratante	moisturising	**tremante**	trembling
incoraggiante	encouraging	**vincente**	winning
martellante	pounding		

Of course, not all '-ing' adjectives will have a corresponding Italian one in **-ante** or **-ente** ('boring' and 'tiring' are **noioso** and **faticoso**, for example), but it's worth trying and then checking with your dictionary.

Now, complete the following sentences:

---

24 **Marina è sempre allegra: il suo viso .... la rende simpatica a tutti.**
Marina is always cheerful: her smiling face makes everyone like her.

25 **Il risultato del sondaggio è stato ....**
The result of the survey has been surprising.

Finally, complete the following sentences with the correct form:

---

26 **............................... la spesa solo ieri, non ho niente in frigo.**
Despite doing the shopping only yesterday, I have nothing in the fridge.

27 **............................... la spesa, ho visto Daniela al supermercato.**
While doing the shopping, I saw Daniela at the supermarket.

28 **Non sei d'accordo che .... la spesa è la cosa più noiosa del mondo?**
Don't you agree that doing the shopping is the most boring thing in the world?

29 **Ieri ho visto Daniela .... la spesa al supermercato.**
Yesterday I saw Daniela doing the shopping at the supermarket.

30 **Dopo .... la spesa, devo assolutamente passare da Daniela.**
After doing the shopping, I really must call on Daniela.

See for further information
Soluzioni!, Chapter 23
A Reference Grammar of Modern Italian, Chapters 14 and 15

Upgrade your vocabulary: Politics and current affairs

DAY 18

To be comfortable when you talk, read or write about politics and current affairs, you need to have sufficient vocabulary relating to both the English-speaking and the Italian contexts. The lexical area is vast, but you can make sure that you know some basic general terms at least.

il governo government
al governo in power, ruling, as in **i partiti al governo,** the parties in power
governare to rule
governativo governmental
il governatore governor

il parlamento parliament
il parlamentare/il deputato member of parliament
la Camera dei Deputati Italian lower house of parliament
il Senato Senate, Italian upper house of parliament
il senatore senator

il voto vote
votare to vote
a favore di in favour of, for
contro against

il candidato candidate
candidarsi to stand for election

le elezioni politiche, amministrative general, local election (notice the plural in Italian)
eleggere to elect
l'elettore voter
l'elettorato the electorate
elettorale election (adj.), as in **la campagna elettorale** election campaign and **la lista elettorale** list of candidates

---

1 Guess the meaning of **la Camera dei Comuni:**

....

2 Guess 'the House of Lords':

—— ——————— ——— ————

il potere power (as in **il potere politico**, political power)
il partito party (political)
la partitocrazia hijacking of institutions by political parties
la politica politics, policy
l'uomo politico politician
i politici politicians

---

3   Guess the meaning of **i partiti di estrema destra:**
....

4   Guess 'the parties of the left':
i_____ ___ _____

5   Guess 'the centre parties':
i_____ ___ _____

---

la maggioranza majority, as in **un governo di maggioranza**
    a majority government
essere in maggioranza to be in the majority
maggioritario majority (adj.), as in **il sistema maggioritario**
    first-past-the-post system

la minoranza minority
minoritario minority (adj.)

diventare maggiorenne to come of age
essere minorenne to be under age

---

6   Guess the meaning of **la maggioranza silenziosa:**
....

7   Guess the meaning of **le minoranze etniche:**
....

8   Guess 'the minority parties':
i_____ ___ _____

9   Guess 'the majority of Italians':
la _____ degli _____

la legge law
legale legal, lawful
leale loyal
entrare in vigore to come into force

il bilancio budget
la finanziaria finance act, budget

il trattato/il patto treaty
l'accordo agreement
la trattativa negotiation
essere in trattativa to be
  in negotiation
trattare to negotiate, as in
  trattare un affare to
  negotiate a deal

---

10 Guess the meaning of **le trattative di pace:**

....

11 Guess 'peace treaty':
il _ _ _ _ _ _ _ _ _ _   _ _   _ _ _ _ _

---

il (primo) ministro
  (Prime) Minister
il ministero ministry
ministeriale ministerial

la riunione meeting
il comizio political rally
il comitato committee

il Consiglio dei Ministri Council of
Ministers, Cabinet
il Presidente del Consiglio Prime Minister

la manifestazione demonstration
il manifestante/dimostrante demonstrator
il corteo march, demonstration

Now complete the following sentences with the missing words:

---

12 A che ora è stato raggiunto _ ' _ _ _ _ _ _ _ _ sul _ _ _ _ _ _ _ _ dell'Unione
Europea?
At what time was the agreement on the EU budget reached?

13 Per chi _ _ _ _ _ _ _ alle _ _ _ _ _ _ _ _ _ _ _ _ _ _ _ _ _ _?
Who will you be voting for in the general election?

14 – 15 È difficile per il _ _ _ _ _ _ _ _ _ _ _ _ _ di un _ _ _ _ _ _ _ di
_ _ _ _ _ _ _ _ imporre il programma legislativo che ha promesso
all' _ _ _ _ _ _ _ _ _ _.
*It is hard for the Prime Minister of a minority government to
push through the legislative programme that he has promised
the electorate.*

la democrazia democracy
democratico democratic
antidemocratico undemocratic

la monarchia monarchy
monarchico monarchic,
  monarchist
il/la sovrano/-a monarch,
  sovereign

il proletariato/la classe operaia
  working class
proletario working-class (adj.),
  proletarian
il proletario working-class person

il Partito Laburista Labour
  Party (GB)
il laburismo Labour movement
il/la laburista Labour supporter
  or party member

il Partito Comunista
  Communist Party

il comunismo communism
il/la comunista communist

il Partito Socialista Socialist Party
il socialismo socialism
il/la socialista socialist

Il Partito Conservatore
  Conservative Party (GB)
il conservatorismo Conservatism
il conservatore/la conservatrice
  Conservative supporter or party
  member

l'aristocrazia aristocracy
aristocratico aristocratic

la borghesia middle class
borghese middle-class (adj.),
  bourgeois

lo stato state
statale state (adj.), as in
  le sovvenzioni statali, state
  subsidies

---

16 Guess the meaning of **la sovranità popolare:**
....

17 Guess the meaning of **aspirazioni piccolo borghesi:**
....

Try to deduce the following:

18 'bureaucratic':

— — — — — — — — — —

19 'dictator':
un — — — — — — — — —

20 'dictatorial':

— — — — — — — — — — —

21 'anarchy':
l' — — — — — — —

la cittadinanza citizenship, nationality
l'identità nazionale national identity
il nazionalismo nationalism
i diritti civili civil rights
i doveri del cittadino civic duties

il sindacato trade union
il sindacalista trade unionist
il sindaco mayor

---

22 Guess 'civil rights movement':

il _ _ _ _ _ _ _ _ _ _ _ per i _ _ _ _ _ _ _

_ _ _ _ _ _ _

23 Guess 'identity card':

la _ _ _ _ _ _ d' _ _ _ _ _ _ _ _ _

Now translate the following sentences into English:

24 – 25 Il conservatorismo britannico ha ben poco in comune con la destra
politica degli Stati Uniti.

....

....

26 – 28 In fin dei conti è un seguace delle tendenze di destra del suo partito,
nonostante il suo passato di esponente del centro-sinistra.

....

....

29 – 30 I sindacati dei lavoratori hanno perduto gran parte del potere di cui
godevano negli Anni 70.

....

....

Do you find imperatives confusing, particularly when a pronoun is needed as well? Italian imperatives are really quite straightforward, once you have found your way around them and have had sufficient practice. The exercises in this chapter will help you get your imperatives (and your pronouns!) right every time.

I   Forms that differ from other verbal forms

Nearly all forms of the imperative are identical to other verbal forms that you know already: the **noi** and **voi** forms are identical to the present indicative; the **Lei** form to the present subjunctive; the **tu** form of **-ere** and **-ire** verbs is also identical to the present indicative. So, the only new ones are the **tu** form of **-are** verbs and the negative imperative of the **tu** form, which is like the infinitive. The following table shows all regular imperatives, with the new forms in bold:

	-are comprare to buy	**-ere vendere** to sell	**-ire finire** to finish	**aprire** to open
tu	**compra**	vendi	finisci	apri
	non comprare	**non vendere**	**non finire**	**non aprire**
Lei	compri	venda	finisca	apra
	non compri	non venda	non finisca	non apra
noi	compriamo	vendiamo	finiamo	apriamo
	non compriamo	non vendiamo	non finiamo	non apriamo
voi	comprate	vendete	finite	aprite
	non comprate	non vendete	non finite	non aprite

Any pronoun will be attached to the **tu**, **noi** and **voi** forms and precede the **Lei** forms. In the case of the negative **tu** forms, the last **-e** of the infinitive will disappear. Here are some examples:

> **Compra la frutta! Comprala!**
> [Buy the fruit. Buy it.]
> **Compra il formaggio! Compralo!**
> [Buy the cheese. Buy it.]

Non comprare le fragole! Non comprarle!
[Don't buy the strawberries. Don't buy them.]
Non comprare i funghi! Non comprarli!
[Don't buy the mushrooms. Don't buy them.]
Vendi la macchina a Paolo! Vendigliela!
[Sell your car to Paolo. Sell it to him.]
Non vendere il motorino a Francesca! Non venderglielo!
[Don't sell your moped to Francesca. Don't sell it to her.]
Apri la porta a me! Aprimi la porta! Aprimela!
[Open the door to me. Open it to me.]
Apriamo le finestre per la mamma! Apriamogliele!
[Let's open the windows for mum. Let's open them for her.]
Signor Rossi, non compri questa macchina per suo figlio! Non gliela compri!
[Mr Rossi, don't buy this car for your son. Don't buy it for him.]

Rewrite the following imperatives, replacing the underlined words with the correct pronoun(s), as in the example:

Ex. Compriamo una bicicletta.
Let's buy a bicycle.
Compriamola!
Let's buy it.

1 Comprate questo libro per Luigi!
Buy this book for Luigi.
....!
Buy it for him.

2 Compri questi guanti per Sua moglie!
Buy these gloves for your wife.
....!
Buy them for her.

3 Compra un gelato a noi!
Buy an ice-cream for us.
....!
Buy it for us.

4 Vendi una di queste piante a me!
Sell one of these plants to me.
.... una!
Sell me one of them.

5 Non vendiamo il motorino a Giulia!
Let's not sell our moped to Giulia.
....!
Let's not sell it to her.

6 Finisci uno di questi libri!
Finish one of these books.
.... uno!
Finish one of them.

7 Aprite la porta al postino!
Open the door to the postman.
.... la porta!
Open the door to him.

8 Non apriamo nessuno di questi pacchi!
Let's not open any of these parcels.
.... nessuno!
Let's not open any of them.

II   The imperative of irregular verbs

Verbs which have irregular present tenses will also have irregular imperatives, but the imperatives of the **tu**, **noi** and **voi** forms will be identical to the verb's present tense, while the imperative of the **Lei** form will be identical to that of its present subjunctive, so there are no new forms to learn. Pronouns will be joined to the imperatives according to the rule in Section I.

Rewrite the following imperatives, replacing the underlined words with the correct pronoun(s):

> **9** Bevi il latte!   .... !
> *Drink your milk.*   *Drink it.*
>
> **10** Beviamoci una birra insieme!   .... una insieme!
> *Let's have a beer together.*   *Let's have one together.*
>
> **11** Non bevete troppo vino!   .... troppo!
> *Don't drink too much wine.*   *Don't drink too much of it.*
>
> **12** Scegliete voi il regalo per Laura!   .... voi!
> *You choose the present for Laura.*   *You choose it for her.*
>
> **13** Scelga uno di questi premi!   .... uno!
> *Choose one of these prizes.*   *Choose one of them.*
>
> **14** Non togliermi il libro di mano.   .... di mano!
> *Don't take the book from my hands.* *Don't take it from my hands.*
>
> **15** Tenga stretto quel cane!   .... stretto!
> *Hold that dog tight.*   *Hold it tight.*
>
> **16** Tieni questo pacco per me un momento! .... un momento!
> *Hold this parcel for me for a second.* *Hold it for me for a second.*

III   Verbs with irregular imperatives

Only eight verbs have irregular imperatives, but only in their **tu** form and, for some of them, in their **voi** forms. The **noi** form is like these verbs' present indicative and the **Lei** form like their present subjunctive. Here is a table of these imperatives, with the irregular forms in bold:

Infinitive	tu	voi	Lei
avere	**abbi**	**abbiate**	abbia
essere	**sii**	**siate**	sia
sapere	**sappi**	**sappiate**	sappia
stare	**sta'*/stai**	state	stia

Infinitive	tu	voi	Lei
andare	va'*/vai	andate	vada
dare	da'*/dai	date	dia
dire	di'*	dite	dica
fare	fa'*/fai	fate	faccia

Once again, any pronouns required will be joined to the imperatives according to the rule in Section I. When the five asterisked imperatives are joined to any pronoun, except **gli**, the initial consonant of this pronoun is doubled, as in:

> **Da' questo libro a me! Dallo a me! Dammi questo libro! Dammelo!**
> [Give this book to me. Give it to me. Give me this book. Give me it.]
> **Da' questa rivista alla mamma! Dalla a lei! Dalle questa rivista! Dagliela!**
> [Give this magazine to your mum. Give it to her. Give her this magazine. Give her it.]

Rewrite the following imperatives, replacing the underlined words with the correct pronoun(s):

17 Sta' a sentire <u>tuo fratello</u>!   .... a sentire!
Listen to your brother.   *Listen to him.*

18 Non abbia paura <u>del cane</u>!   .... paura!
Don't be afraid of the dog.   *Don't be afraid if it.*

19 Non essere gelosa <u>di tua sorella</u>!   .... gelosa!
Don't be jealous of your sister.   *Don't be jealous of her.*

20 Di' la verità <u>a me</u>!   .... la verità!
Tell the truth to me.   *Tell me the truth.*

21 Di' <u>questo</u> <u>a Paolo</u>!   ....!
Tell this to Paolo.   *Tell him it.*

22 Dite <u>questo</u> <u>a noi</u>!   ....!
Tell this to us.   *Tell us it.*

23 Va' <u>a fare la spesa</u>!   ....!
Go and do the shopping.   *Go there.*

24 Fa' un favore a me!
Do a favour to me.

.... un favore!
Do me a favour.

25 Fa' questo per noi!
Do this for us.

...........................!
Do it for us.

26 Da' questa lettera a noi!
Give this letter to us.

...........................!
Give it to us.

27 Date uno di questi libri a noi!
Give one of these books to us.

.... uno!
Give us one of them.

28 Dia quelle riviste a loro!
Give those magazines to them.

...........................!
Give them to them.

29 Mi faccia sapere questo!
Let me know this.

.... sapere!
Let me know it.

30 Non dica questo a Luisa!
Don't tell this to Luisa.

...........................!
Don't tell her it.

See for further information
Soluzioni!, Chapter 22
A Reference Grammar of Modern Italian, Chapter 14

This is obviously a huge lexical area, but, to make it easier, this chapter will focus on relatively painless ways of expanding your vocabulary using the techniques you have learnt over the past days: linking unfamiliar words to more familiar cognates and guessing intelligently. Fortunately, complicated technical words are very often the easiest to guess, once you have a feel for the ending and the gender to go for.

la scienza science
lo/la scienziato/-a scientist
scientifico scientific
coscienza conscience, awareness, consciousness
coscienzioso conscientious

la fisica physics
il/la fisico/-a physicist
fisico physical
il fisico physique

1 Guess 'metaphysical':

_ _ _ _ _ _ _ _ _ _ _/**-a**

2 Guess 'nuclear physics':

_ _ _ _ _ _ _ _ _ _ _ _ _ _ _ _

la chimica chemistry

chimico chemical
il prodotto chimico chemical (n.)

3 Guess 'a chemist' (compare the relationship between **la fisica** and **il/la fisico/a**):
un/una _ _ _ _ _ _ _/ **-a** (chemistry expert, not a pharmacist)

la genetica genetics
il/la genetista geneticist

genetico genetic
il gene gene

il genio genius
avere un colpo di genio to have
  a brainwave
geniale brilliant, of genius

4 Guess the meaning of **l'ingegneria genetica:**

....

ingegnere engineer
l'ingegno intelligence, talent, ingenuity
ingegnoso clever, ingenious

la biologia biology   **biologico** biological   **il/la biologo/-a** biologist

Based on the 'biology' pattern, complete the following series of terms for 'astrology', 'anthropology' and 'psychology':

5 astrology   l'_ _ _ _ _ _ _ _ _ _
    astrological   _ _ _ _ _ _ _ _ _ _ _
    astrologer   l'_ _ _ _ _ _ _ _ _ / -a

6 anthropology   l' *antro*_ _ _ _ _ _ _
    anthropological _ _ _ _ _ _ _ _ _ _ _ _
    anthropologist l'_ _ _ _ _ _ _ _ _ _ _ _ / -a

7 psychology   la *psico* _ _ _ _ _ _
    psychological   _ _ _ _ _ _ _ _ _ _ _
    psychologist   lo/la _ _ _ _ _ _ _ _ _ / -a

You could extend the list to cover other '-ologies', such as **archeologia**, **sociologia**, **teologia**, **geologia**, **etnologia**, and **tecnologia**.

l'esperimento experiment
l'esperienza experience
esperto experienced, expert
sperimentare to experiment
sperimentale experimental
la sperimentazione
  experimentation

provare to test, to prove, to try
  on (clothes)
la prova test, trial (not legal), proof
la provetta test tube

8 Guess the meaning of **i bambini in provetta**:

....

9 Guess the meaning of **allo stadio sperimentale:**

....

il progresso progress, advance
fare progressi to make progress
progredire to progress
progressista progressive (person or attitude)

l'indagine (f.) investigation, research
indagare to investigate

il progetto plan, project
il progetto di legge bill (proposed law)
progettare to plan
la progettazione planning
la ricerca research
il ricercatore/la ricercatrice researcher

10 Guess 'a market survey':
un' __ __ __ __ __ __ __ __ di mercato

Now complete the following sentences with the missing words:

11 Anche se non era __ __ __ __ __ __ , era __ __ __ __ __ __ __ __ __ __ __ e prendeva sempre voti discreti.
Although she was not a genius, she was conscientious and always had reasonable marks.

12 Ma come puoi credere all'__ __ __ __ __ __ __ __ __ __?
How can you believe in astrology?

13 I __ __ __ __ __ __ __ __ di __ __ __ __ __ __ __ scientifica sono a volte molto costosi ed è perciò abbastanza difficile ottenere i finanziamenti necessari.
Scientific research projects are sometimes very costly and it is therefore quite difficult to secure the necessary funding.

14 - **15** I __ __ __ __ __ __ __ __ __ della __ __ __ __ __ __ __ __ fanno paura ad alcuni, che li paragonano agli __ __ __ __ __ __ __ __ __ __ __ del dottor Frankenstein.
Advances in genetics frighten some people, who compare them to Dr Frankenstein's experiments.

l'ambiente (m.) environment
ambientale environmental
ambientalista environmentalist
l'inquinamento pollution
   inquinamento atmosferico air pollution
              acustico noise pollution
              idrico water pollution
              marino sea pollution
              radioattivo nuclear pollution
inquinare to pollute
inquinante polluting
la contaminazione contamination
contaminare to contaminate

ecologia ecology, environmental science
ecologico environmentally friendly

la salvaguardia protection
salvaguardare to protect, safeguard
il livello di guardia danger level
       di sicurezza safety level
       di sopportazione tolerance level

---

16 Guess the meaning of **il degrado ambientale:**

....

17 Guess the meaning of **la pelliccia ecologica:**

....

18 Guess 'environmental impact':
  l'_ _ _ _ _ _ _   _ _ _ _ _ _ _ _ _ _

---

la foresta forest
la deforestazione deforestation

il buco nell'ozono the hole in the ozone layer
la serra greenhouse
i clorofluorocarburi CFC gases
la centrale elettrica power station
          nucleare nuclear power station

le scorie radioattive (f.pl.) nuclear waste

il bosco wood
disboscamento deforestation

l'anidride carbonica carbon dioxide
i combustibili fossili fossil fuel
l'energia solare solar power

19 Guess the meaning of **l'effetto-serra:**
....

20 Guess the meaning of **la foresta pluviale:**
....

21 Guess 'acid rain':
la __ __ __ __ __ __ __   __ __ __ __ __

---

la spazzatura rubbish
i rifiuti (pl.) waste
gli scarichi (pl.) liquid,
  chemical waste
la discarica land-fill site
l'inceneritore incinerator
incenerire to incinerate

lo smaltimento disposal
smaltire to dispose of
il riciclaggio recycling
riciclare to recycle
la raccolta differenziata pre-sorted
  rubbish collection

---

22 Guess the meaning of **gli scarichi industriali:**
....

23 Guess the meaning of **i rifiuti tossici:**
....

24 Guess 'biodegradable':
__ __ __ __ __ __ __ __ __ __ __ __ __

25 Guess 'pesticides':
i __ __ __ __ __ __ __ __ __

26 Guess the meaning of **l'equilibrio biologico:**
....

27 Guess the meaning of **le mutazioni climatiche:**
....

28 Guess 'GM products':
i prodotti modi __ __ __ __ __ __   __ __ __ __ __ __ __ __ __ __ __ __ __ __

Now complete the following sentences with the missing words:

29 Mi preoccupano molto le questioni _ _ _ _ _ _ _ _ _ _ , particolarmente quello
che dicono gli _ _ _ _ _ _ _ _ _ _ sull' _ _ _ _ _ _ _ - _ _ _ _ _ .
*Environmental issues worry me a great deal, particularly what
scientists tell us about the greenhouse effect.*

30 L' _ _ _ _ _ _ _ _ _ _ _ _ del Mediterraneo, specialmente quello causato
da chiazze di petrolio e da _ _ _ _ _ _ _ _ chimici e industriali, è una vera
tragedia.
*The pollution of the Mediterranean, especially that caused by oil
slicks and by chemical and industrial waste, is a real tragedy.*

Key points:
Impersonal and passive
constructions with *si*

Impersonal constructions are used very frequently in Italian, particularly when the person doing the action is not as important as the action itself, or when the action applies to people in general. This chapter will help you get your impersonal constructions right and improve your style by using them more frequently.

I   Basic impersonal constructions

These are done with **si** and the third person of the verb, in any tense. The equivalent English sentence will have 'one' or 'people' as an impersonal or general subject, or, much more frequently, the 'you' which does not refer to a specific person but to everyone in general. Here are some examples:

Si parla molto bene del nuovo film di Mel Gibson.
[People speak very highly of Mel Gibson's new film.]
A che ora si mangia a casa tua?
[At what time do you eat in your house?]
Si pensava che il cane fosse stato rubato.
[We/they thought that the dog had been stolen.]
È una storia troppo complicata, non si capisce niente!
[The story is too complex, one can't understand anything!]

Very often, a transitive verb is used with an object, as in:

Come si scrive il tuo cognome?
[How do you spell your surname?]
Dove si comprano i biglietti dell'autobus?
[Where does one buy bus tickets?]
Ieri sera si vedevano tantissime stelle.
[Last night you could see very many stars.]

In this case, the verb will need to match this noun in number: if the noun is plural, the verb will be in the third person plural. This type of sentence is like a passive one and can have a passive meaning in English, too:

L'affitto si paga ogni mese. = L'affitto è pagato ogni mese.
[The rent is paid every month.]
Quando si organizzerebbero le prossime riunioni? = Quando sarebbero organizzate le prossime riunioni?
[When would the next meetings be arranged?]

Anche quest'anno le elezioni si terranno a giugno. =
Anche quest'anno le elezioni saranno tenute a giugno.
[This year too, the elections will be held in June.]
Tutti pensano che si paghino troppe tasse.
[Everyone thinks that too many taxes are paid/that we pay too many taxes.]

In the following sentences, choose the correct form of the verb:

> **1** Alla conferenza si parlerà/parleranno delle nuove tendenze letterarie.
> *At the conference we shall talk about the new literary trends.*
>
> **2** Si vede/vedono molti ragazzi vestiti tutti di nero.
> *One sees many youngsters dressed entirely in black.*
>
> **3** Finalmente si firmerà/firmeranno i nuovi contratti di lavoro.
> *The new work contracts will be signed at last.*
>
> **4** In passato non si ricevevano/riceveva così tanta pubblicità per posta.
> *In the past we didn't receive so much advertising by post.*
>
> **5** Vorrei sapere come si fa/fanno dei dolci così buoni!
> *I'd like to know how one makes cakes as nice as these!*
>
> **6** Ma come si fa/fanno a parcheggiare in questo modo!
> *How can people park in this way!*

II Using *si* with modal and reflexive verbs

When this construction is used with verbs like **dovere**, **potere**, **volere**, **sapere** (when it means 'to be able to'), you need to be more careful, because the accompanying noun will not be immediately after the modal verb but will affect it. Look at these examples:

Dove si devono consegnare questi documenti?
[Where must these documents be handed in?]
Se si vogliono comprare dei mobili antichi a poco prezzo, si possono provare le aste.
[If one wants to buy antique furniture cheaply, one can try the auctions.]
Si può mettere in lavatrice questo vestito?
[Can this dress be put in the washing machine?]

If there is no noun, the modal verb will be in the third person singular:

Si deve rispondere entro domani.
[One must reply by tomorrow.]

Non si poteva parlare a voce alta.
[One could not speak loudly.]
Dopo il corso, si saprà cavalcare con disinvoltura.
[After the course, people will be able to ride with confidence.]

When this construction is used with reflexive or reciprocal verbs, which already have a **si** in their third persons, you need to add **ci**. Here are some examples:

Quando ci si incontrava per la strada, ci si salutava con una stretta di mano.
[When people met in the street, they would greet each other with a handshake.]
Con i tuoi amici ci si diverte sempre un sacco.
[With your friends, we always have a really good time.]
Che seccatura, quando ci si dimentica qualcosa di importante!
[How annoying, when one forgets something important!]
Con questo biglietto ci si potrà sedere sia in platea che in galleria.
[With this ticket people will be able to sit either in the stalls or in the circle.]

Complete the following sentences:

---

7 Quando si è a dieta, ... (dover fare) anche un po' di ginnastica.
When you are on a diet, you should do a bit of exercise, too.

8 In questa città .... (annoiarsi) da morire.
In this town we get bored to tears.

9 Quello stereo .... (poter comprare) a meno al centro commerciale.
That hi-fi system could have been bought more cheaply from the shopping centre.

10 Per star bene, ... (dover mangiare) più frutta.
To be healthy, one should eat more fruit.

11 Se .... (volersi riposare) veramente, non c'è niente di meglio di una bella vacanza!
If you really want a rest, there's nothing better than a good holiday!

12 Probabilmente in futuro .... (sposarsi) più tardi.
In the future, people will probably marry later in life.

III   Using the *si* construction with adjectives

Some verbs can be followed by an adjective or a noun which is necessary to complete their meaning. The most frequently used of these verbs are: **essere**, **diventare**, **rimanere**, **sentirsi** and **stare**. If these are used in the construction with **si**, the following adjective or noun must be plural, even if the verb is singular and masculine, unless the context is obviously feminine.

Look at the following examples:

In Italia si diventa medici solo dopo molti anni di studio.
[In Italy one becomes a doctor only after many years of study.]
Se non ci si sente adatti ad un lavoro o non si è portati per una materia di studio, è molto meglio cambiarli.
[If one does not feel suited to a job or cut out for a school subject, it is much better to change them.]
Quando si è distratti come te, è normale perdere le cose.
[When one is as scatty as you are, it's normal to lose things.]
Anche se si è donne, non si dovrebbe essere sfruttate!
[Despite being a woman, one should not be exploited!]

Rewrite the following sentences using the **si** construction:

---

13 **Quando uno si sente depresso, deve fare uno sforzo per condurre una vita normale.**
When you feel depressed, you must make an effort to lead a normal life.

....

14 **Non credi anche tu che d'inverno uno si senta più stanco?**
Don't you think that in the winter one feels more tired?

....

15 **Dovresti essere disposto ad accettare il punto di vista altrui anche se non sei contento della situazione.**
You should be able to accept someone else's point of view even if you are not happy with the situation.

....

16 **Pensavo che tutti si sentissero più buoni a Natale!**
I thought that everyone felt kinder at Christmas!

....

17 **Vi ritenete fortunati di essere nati in questo secolo?**
Do you consider yourselves lucky to have been born in this century?

....

> **18** **La chirurgia plastica è la soluzione estrema se una donna è insoddisfatta del proprio aspetto.**
> *Plastic surgery is the ultimate solution if a woman is unhappy with her appearance.*
>
> ....

IV   Using the *si* construction in compound tenses

In compound tenses (i.e. **passato prossimo**, pluperfect, compound conditional, etc.), the auxiliary in constructions with **si** is always **essere**.

The rules for the agreement of the past participle are very straightforward:

- If there is an object, the past participle will agree with this noun in gender and number. For example, the past tense of **dalla finestra si vedono passare le gondole** [One can see the gondolas go by from the window] is **dalla finestra si sono viste passare le gondole** [One saw the gondolas go by from the window].
- If there is no object, the participle of a verb which normally takes **avere** will be masculine singular. For example, the compound form of **si mangerebbe meglio fuori** [One would eat better out] is **si sarebbe mangiato meglio fuori** [One would have eaten better out] (i.e. **mangiato** is masculine singular because the usual auxiliary of **mangiare** is **avere**).
- The participle of a verb which normally takes **essere** (i.e. intransitive and reflexive verbs) will be masculine plural. For example, the past tense of **si diventa sempre più indifferenti alla sofferenza** [One becomes ever more indifferent to suffering] is **si è diventati sempre più indifferenti alla sofferenza** [One has become ever more indifferent to suffering]; the past tense of **ci si avvicina timidamente alla filosofia** [One approaches philosophy apprehensively] is **ci si è avvicinati timidamente alla filosofia** [One has approached philosophy apprehensively].

Here are some more examples:

> **Alla riunione si è discusso di tutto, meno che delle cose veramente importanti!**
> [Everything was discussed at the meeting, except the really important things!]
> **Si era pensato di partire presto per evitare il traffico.**
> [We/they had thought of leaving early to avoid the traffic.]
> **Tutti pensano che si siano pagate troppe tasse quest'anno.**
> [Everyone thinks that too many taxes have been paid this year.]
> **Con questo biglietto ci si è potuti sedere in prima classe.**
> [With this ticket people have been able to sit in the first-class seats.]

Senza il suo aiuto, si sarebbe impazziti a trovare la strada giusta.
[Without his help, one would have gone mad finding the right route.]

Now, put the verbs in the following sentences in their compound form:

---

19 **Le spese non si pagano mai in contanti.**
The expenses are never paid in cash.
....
The expenses have never been paid in cash.

20 **Quando si terrebbe questa riunione?**
When would this meeting be held?
....
When would this meeting have been held?

21 **In questo libro non si capisce niente.**
One can't understand anything in this book.
....
One has not been able to understand anything in this book.

22 **Per perdere peso si dovrebbe fare più ginnastica.**
To lose weight, one should do more exercise.
....
To lose weight, one should have done more exercise.

23 **Purtroppo non si ha il tempo di discutere la faccenda.**
Unfortunately one has no time to discuss the matter.
....
Unfortunately one has had no time to discuss the matter.

V   Using the construction with *si*

This construction is very widely used in Italian, especially whenever the action itself is more important than the person doing it, when giving instructions or directions, for example, or when we are speaking generally about what happens or has happened. It is also widely used in advertising, because it is quick and immediate. Make a conscious effort to use it more often: instead of thinking in terms of **è necessario** or **bisogna** to express need, next time try **si deve**; when you want to say **è possibile**, try saying **si può**. When telling people how something is done, say **si prende**, **si gira**, **si piega**, **si mescola**, **si taglia**, **si preme questo pulsante**, etc.

The more you use it, the easier it gets and the more idiomatic your Italian will be: **si fanno miracoli con un po' di buona volontà**!

The following set of sentences talks about the journalist's profession. Try saying the same things using the construction with **si**. For further practice, you can try doing the same about other occupations or jobs, like policeman, plumber, model, doctor.

---

24 Se vuoi diventare giornalista, devi andare facilmente d'accordo con la gente.

....

25 È importante che tu sappia memorizzare e riprodurre bene molte informazioni.

....

26 È indispensabile che tu sia disposto a lavorare per molte ore, anche di notte.

....

27 Potrai fare carriera se sarai veloce, accurato e originale quando scriverai gli articoli.

....

28 Quando avrai lavorato per un giornale o una stazione televisiva per parecchi anni, avrai la possibilità di viaggiare e di vivere all'estero.

....

29 Conoscerai persone importanti e persone qualunque.

....

30 Sarai uno strumento di diffusione dell'informazione e di comunicazione.

....

See for further information
Soluzioni!, Chapter 25
A Reference Grammar of Modern Italian, Chapters 6 and 14

Upgrade your vocabulary: Education

This is a useful topic to be familiar with, first of all because you are studying yourself and secondly because it is always a hot political and social issue both in the English-speaking world and in Italy.

la scuola school
>   **a scuola** at/in/to school (note the preposition used; cf. also **a casa** at home/home; **a teatro** at/to the theatre)
>   **uscire di scuola** to come out of school
>   **tagliare/marinare la scuola** to bunk off school
>   **la scuola elementare/primaria** primary school
>>   **media** middle school
>>   **secondaria/superiore** secondary school
>   **la scuola materna/l'asilo** nursery school
>   **la scuola serale** night school

---

1 Guess 'state school':

—— ———— ————

---

scolare/scolastico adj. for school as in **bambini in età scolare** children of school age, and **il programma scolastico** the school curriculum
lo/la scolaro/-a, l'alunno/a pupil (in primary school)
il/la maestro/-a teacher (in primary school)
il professore/la professoressa teacher (all levels above primary school)
il/la docente university lecturer
l'insegnante (m. and f.) teacher (all levels)

2 Guess teaching, as in 'the teaching of history' (compare the relationship between **pagare** to pay, and **pagamento** payment):

— — — — — — — — — — — — — — **della storia**

la classe classroom, year, as in **compito in classe** class test and **Che classe fai?** What year are you in?
essere il primo della classe to be top of the class
il/la compagno/-a di classe/di scuola class/schoolmate
la sezione form, as in **In che sezione sei?** What form are you in?

3 Guess 'flatmate':

il/la _ _ _ _ _ _ _ _ / _ _ _ _ _ _ _ _ _ _ _ _ _ _ _

la lezione class, lesson, as in **Ho lezione d'inglese, di pianoforte, di matematica** … I have an English, piano, maths lesson
far lezione to teach, lecture
lezione universitaria university lecture
la lettura a reading passage, the act of reading (NB false friend, *not* 'a lecture')
ripassare, fare il ripasso to revise (subjects, notes), to do revision
materie di studio school subjects, like **informatica, applicazioni tecniche, educazione artistica**, IT, DT, art
essere bravo in to be good at a school subject, as in **Sono bravissimo in matematica** I am dead good at maths
essere portato per to be talented in, to have an aptitude for
essere negato per/in to be hopeless at
andar bene/male a scuola to do well/badly at school
essere un/a secchione/-a to be a swot
essere assente/presente to be absent/present
assentarsi to absent, excuse oneself
l'assenteismo absenteeism

4 Guess 'private lesson':

la _ _ _ _ _ _ _ _ _ _ _ _ _ _ _

5 Guess 'material':

il _ _ _ _ _ _ _ _ _ _

la facoltà faculty
il liceo secondary school, college
l'istituto tecnico technical secondary school, technical college
il collegio boarding school (NB false friend, *not* 'a college')
il/la collega colleague
l'università university
universitario adj. for university, as in **il settore universitario** the university sector, **i corsi universitari** university courses and **il CUS (Centro Universitario Sportivo)**

---

6 Guess 'mental faculties' (be careful with the agreement!):
le _ _ _ _ _ _ _ _   _ _ _ _ _ _ _ _

7 Guess 'universal':
_ _ _ _ _ _ _ _ _ _ _

---

lo studente/la studentessa student
studentesco adj. for student, as in **la vita studentesca** student life and **il circolo studentesco** the students' union
studiare to study, learn (by studying, as in to learn a language, a musical instrument, etc.), to work (when used for studying, as in **Dovrai studiare di più se vorrai superare gli esami** You'll have to work harder if you want to pass your exams)
lo studio studio, study

---

8 Guess 'studious':
_ _ _ _ _ _ _ _ _

Now complete the following sentences with the missing words:

---

9 - **10** In quanti eravate _ _ _ _ _ _ _ _ alla _ _ _ _ _ _ _ _ _ _ _ _ _ _ _ _?
How many were in your class at primary school?

11 - **12** La vita _ _ _ _ _ _ _ _ _ _ _ _ non è fatta solo di _ _ _ _ _ _.
Student life is not just made of studying.

13 - **15** Nelle _, gli esami sono corretti
dallo stesso _ _ _ _ _ _ _ _ che ha tenuto _ _ _ _ _ _ _ _ _.
In university faculties, exams are marked by the same lecturer who did the lectures.

16 - 18 Negli _ _ _ _ _ _ _ _   _ _ _ _ _ _ _   _ _ _ _ _ _ _ **non si deve portare**
la divisa, ma nei _ _ _ _ _   _ _ _ _ _ _ _ _ e in alcuni _ _ _ _ _ _ _ sì.
*In state technical schools you don't have to wear a uniform, but in
private secondary schools and in some boarding schools you do.*

19 - 21 Tutti i mercoledì Luca _ _ _ _ _ _ _ _ _ _ _ _ _ _ _ _ _ con un _ _ _ _ _ _ _ _ _
_ _ _ _ _ _ _ _ per evitare _ _ _ _ _ _ _ _ _ _ _ _ _ _ _ _ _ _ _ .
*Every Wednesday Luke bunks off school with a classmate
to avoid their chemistry lesson.*

22 - 24 Quando andava a scuola mio padre, _   _ _ _ _ _ _ _ _ _ _ _ non
esisteva. Doveva _ _ _ _ _ _ _ _   _ _ _ _ _ _ _ _ _ _ , ma non _ _ _ _ _ _
molto _ _ _ _ a scuola.
*When my dad was at school there was no IT. He had to
learn philosophy, but didn't do very well at school.*

---

il corso academic course, esp.
  at university
il corso di recupero remedial
  course
seguire/sospendere i corsi to
follow/interrupt one's courses
nel corso di in the course of/
  over/during
correggere to correct, mark

incorreggibile incorrigible
essere bocciato/-a to fail one's
  course/exam
    promosso/-a to pass one's
      course/exam
dare/sostenere un esame
  to take an exam
superare un esame to pass
  an exam

---

25 Guess 'correction':

_ _   _ _ _ _ _ _ _ _ _ _ _ _

26 Guess 'correct':

_ _ _ _ _ _ _ _ _ _

---

la maturità A-level
il diploma certificate, diploma, as in
  il diploma di maturità A-level
  certificate
la laurea degree
laurearsi to graduate, get a degree
essere laureato/-a to be a
  graduate, have a degree
il voto mark

a pieni voti with top marks
prendere bei/brutti voti to get
  good/bad marks
prendere in giro to tease
la pagella school report
gli appunti notes (NB false
  friend: **le note** musical notes)
prendere appunti to take notes
notare to notice

numero di matricola registration number

l'orario timetable
Era ora! About time too!
il banco desk
la cartella school bag
lo zainetto back pack
la cattedra teacher's desk
l'interrogazione viva, oral test

l'intervallo break (in the school day)
la frequenza obbligatoria/ facoltativa compulsory/ optional attendance
l'istruzione education (NB false friend: **educazione** means upbringing, good manners)

---

27 Guess 'educational, instructive':

— — — — — — — — — —

Now complete the following crossword puzzle with the Italian for the following words (the words you need are either words you have learnt today or can be easily guessed from words you have come across today):

'to attend' (11 letters)   'notes' (7 letters)
'to examine' (9 letters)   'registration' (9 letters)
'graduate' (m.s., 8 letters)   'to remedy' (10 letters)

Check your answers against the answer section, then award yourself half a point for each correct answer, for a maximum total of three points.

Key points: Conditional sentences

DAY 23

Conditional (or hypothetical) sentences are a nice, self-contained use of subjunctive and conditional. If used correctly, they immediately lift the standard of your Italian to a higher level. This chapter will help you get your conditional constructions right and improve your style by using them more frequently.

I   When *se* does not introduce a conditional sentence

Before tackling the various types of conditional sentence, you need to be able to distinguish between the use of **se** in conditional sentences and the use of **se** to introduce an indirect or reported question. For example:

> **Mia madre mi ha chiesto se potevo lavarle la macchina.**
> [My mother asked me if (= whether) I could wash her car.]
> **Non sapevo con certezza se avrei avuto tempo di farlo.**
> [I did not know for sure if (= whether) I would have time to do it.]

In both examples, **se** introduces a reported or indirect question, not a conditional one. This essentially means that the sentences above could be turned into direct questions:

> – **Puoi lavarmi la macchina? – mi ha chiesto mia madre.**
> – **Avrò il tempo di farlo? – mi domandavo ma non sapevo con certezza.**

In practice, when **se** introduces a reported or indirect question, it can be translated into English as 'whether' as well as 'if'. **Se** in a conditional sentence, however, can only be translated as 'if'. This is a quick and easy way of double-checking, if you are not sure.

In the following sentences, identify the cases where **se** introduces a conditional sentence (C) and the cases where **se** introduces an indirect question (Q). Mark the sentences (C) or (Q) as appropriate:

---

1 *Se ho tempo, gli darò una mano.*
If I have time, I'll give him a hand.

2 *Mi ha domandato se avrei potuto dargli una mano.*
He asked me if I could give him a hand.

3 **Gli darei una mano, se avessi tempo.**
I would give him a hand if I had time.

4 **Non so se avrò tempo di dargli una mano.**
I don't know if I'll have time to give him a hand.

5 **Gli avrei dato una mano se avessi avuto tempo.**
I would have given him a hand if I had had the time.

6 **Non sapevo se avrei avuto tempo di dargli una mano.**
I didn't know if I would have time to give him a hand.

7 **Se avete tempo, dategli una mano.**
If you have time, give him a hand.

Sometimes, 'if' is used in English to mean 'although' or 'when', as in these examples:

> They were strong, if clumsy.
> As children, we would always play in the streets if it did not rain.

The second example is not a conditional sentence because it really means 'every time/when it was not raining, we played in the streets'. So, if you can replace 'if' with 'whether', 'although' or 'when', the sentence will be straightforward and will not need the tenses used in conditional sentences:

> **Erano forti, anche se maldestri.**
> **Da bambini, giocavamo sempre per la strada se non pioveva.**

II Identifying a conditional sentence and its type
As the name suggests, a conditional sentence makes the doing of one half of the action in the sentence conditional upon the other half. Look at these examples:

(a) If I win the lottery, I'll buy myself a Ferrari.
   (Should I win the lottery, I'll buy myself a Ferrari.)
(b) If I won the lottery, I'd buy myself a Ferrari.
   (Were I to win the lottery, I'd buy myself a Ferrari.)
(c) If I had won the lottery last week, I'd have bought myself a Ferrari.
   (Had I won the lottery last week, I'd have bought myself a Ferrari.)

In all cases, the buying of a Ferrari is conditional upon winning the lottery. If that condition is not met, I keep my old car. Note also the alternative ways in English to express conditional sentences, which do not use the word 'if'.

Identify which type of conditional sentence, (a), (b) or (c), the following exemplify. If a sentence is not a conditional one, mark it with (X):

---

8 If the plumber arrives after 11 o'clock, I'll be out.

9 If you had come before 11, I'd have been here.

10 If we did not sit at the table to eat, our father used to tell us off.

11 It was sunny, even if there were a few clouds to be seen.

12 If I thought you meant that, it would be extremely hurtful.

Once you have identified a conditional sentence and its type, you need to know how that pattern is expressed in Italian. The use of tenses is quite straightforward:

(a) **Se** + present or future indicative in the 'if' clause, present, future or imperative in the main clause.
(b) **Se** + imperfect subjunctive in the 'if' clause, simple conditional (occasionally compound conditional, depending on meaning – see (b) below) in the main clause.
(c) **Se** + pluperfect subjunctive in the 'if' clause, compound conditional (occasionally simple conditional, depending on meaning – see (c) below) in the main clause.

So:

(a) **Se vinco (vincerò) alla lotteria, mi compro (comprerò) una Ferrari.**
(b) **Se vincessi alla lotteria, mi comprerei una Ferrari.**
   Se fossi più fortunata, avrei vinto alla lotteria.
(c) **Se avessi vinto alla lotteria la settimana scorsa, mi sarei comprata (adesso mi comprerei) una Ferrari.**

In practice, type (a) is very like English. So, if the sentence presents a hypothetical outcome, i.e. something that the subject 'would do' or 'would have done', you need to look at types (b) and (c). To discriminate between them, try this method: the outcome will always be expressed by the conditional, simple ('would do') or compound ('would have done'); when the 'if' clause refers to the present or future or is general ('if you were tidy'), use the imperfect subjunctive; when the 'if' clause refers to the past ('if you had been tidy'), use the pluperfect subjunctive.

Remember that the conditional is NEVER used in the **se** clause.

Now complete the following sentences with the correct tense of the verb in brackets:

---

13 *Se tu me lo .... (dire) in tempo, avrei potuto aiutarti.*
If you had told me sooner, I'd have been able to help you.

14 *Se arriviamo in ritardo, i miei .... (arrabbiarsi).*
If we are late, my parents will get angry.

15 *Se ci .... (essere) anche tu qui, ci divertiremmo un mondo insieme!*
If you were here too, we'd have such a great time together!

16 *Se noi .... (potere) aiutarvi, lo faremo volentieri.*
If we could help you, we'd gladly do it.

17 *Hanno detto che .... (andare) anche loro al mare, se ne avessero veramente voglia.*
They said that they would go to the seaside too, if they really felt like it.

18 *Se lei avesse più soldi, ... (comprarsi) una macchina nuova.*
If she had more money, she would buy herself a new car.

19 *Se lo .... (vedere) domani, salutamelo.*
If you see him tomorrow, give him my regards.

20 *Paola, ti .... (invitare), se avessi saputo che eri in città.*
Paola, I would have invited you if I had known that you were in town.

It is also possible to find the combination **se** + **passato prossimo**, as in the following examples:

> **Se ho fatto un errore, mi scuso.**
> [If I have made a mistake, I apologize.]
> **Se ho fatto un errore, mi scuserò.**
> [If I have made a mistake, I will apologize.]
> **Se ho fatto un errore, non l'ho fatto apposta.**
> [If I have made a mistake, I didn't do it on purpose.]

As you can see, these tense patterns are identical to the English ones, too. Note the fundamental difference between:

> **Se facessi un errore, mi scuserei.**
> [If I made (i.e. were to make) a mistake, I would apologize.], a type (b) conditional sentence, and
> **Se ho fatto un errore, mi scuso.**
> [If I have made a mistake, I apologize.]

In the following sentences, choose the correct alternative in the 'if' clause:

---

21 *Se ha perso/perdesse il treno, si arrabbierà tantissimo.*
If he missed the train, he'll be really cross.

22 *Se è mancato/mancasse alla riunione, ce la caveremmo da soli.*
If he missed the meeting, we'd manage on our own.

23 *Se è mancato/mancasse alla riunione, ce la caveremo da soli.*
If he has missed the meeting, we'll manage on our own.

III   One further pattern: the imperfect indicative in type (c)

It is also possible to find, in the spoken language and with modal verbs in particular, that the compound conditional and/or the pluperfect subjunctive of type (c) conditional sentences are replaced by imperfect indicatives, as in the following examples:

Se vincevo alla lotteria, mi compravo una Ferrari.
[Had I won the lottery, I would have bought myself a Ferrari.]
Se volevi uscire, potevi dirlo prima.
[If you (had) wanted to go out, you could have said it sooner.]

Using this pattern, however, does not do anything to improve your style and register, so it is best avoided.

IV   Ring the changes

It is sometimes possible to express a condition by using **in caso di**, **con** or **senza** followed by a noun, as in:

In caso di difficoltà, telefonami!
[In the event of problems (should you have any problems), phone me!]
Senza l'aiuto dei genitori, non avrebbe mai comprato questa casa.
[Without his/her parents' help (if his/her parents had not helped him/her), s/he would never have bought this house.]

A further option is to use a gerund, as we have seen in Day 17, but only if the subject of the 'if' clause is the same as that of the main clause. For example:

Se tu tornassi a casa per le 8, potresti cenare con noi.
Tornando a casa per le 8, potresti cenare con noi.
[If you came back home by 8, you could have dinner with us.
Coming back home by 8, you could have dinner with us.]

Se lo avessimo saputo prima, gli avremmo dato noi una mano.

Avendolo saputo prima, gli avremmo dato noi una mano.

[Had we known about it before, we would have given him a hand. Having known about it before, we would have given him a hand.]

Now, rewrite the following sentences using an alternative to the 'if' clause:

---

24 **Se non si avesse un indirizzo fisso, non si potrebbe trovare lavoro.**
If one didn't have a fixed address, it would be impossible to find a job.
....

25 **Se avessero avuto un po' di fortuna, sarebbero venuti con noi.**
If they had had a bit of luck, they would have come with us.
....

26 **Se ci fosse un incendio, rompete il vetro!**
Should there be a fire, break the glass!
....

V   Being in control and using conditional sentences

Conditional sentences are widely used in Italian, and are an excellent way to 'upgrade' your linguistic standard. Make a conscious effort to use them more often: instead of thinking in terms of: **vado in piscina quando non piove**, next time try: **se piovesse**, **non andrei in piscina**. The more you use them, the easier they get and the more sophisticated your Italian will be.

In the following set of sentences, try saying the same things using a conditional construction. The first sentence has the translation of the conditional version, to guide you.

---

27 **Voglio andare in vacanza, ma non ho i soldi.**
I want to go on holiday, but I have no money.
....
If I had the money, I would go on holiday.

28 **Sii più ottimista, la vita ti sembrerà più bella!**
Be more positive, life will seem better!
....

29 **Non hanno finito di studiare perché sono stufi della matematica.**
They did not finish their work because they are fed up with maths.
....

30 **Fuma tantissimo e per questo tossisce di continuo.**
S/he smokes a great deal and for this reason s/he coughs all the time.

....

See for further information
Soluzioni!, Chapter 21
A Reference Grammar of Modern Italian, Chapter 14

Upgrade your style: Dialogue and reported speech

Narrative (both oral and written) can be greatly livened up and varied by the inclusion of passages of dialogue, provided you can make them interesting by introducing a degree of lexical and stylistic variety.

I Dialogue and reported speech: alternatives to *dire*, *pensare* and *rispondere*

There is a very wide range of verbs in Italian which can be used to report speech and thoughts, and if you make a conscious effort to ring the changes on overused verbs such as **dire**, **pensare**, and **rispondere**, you can make an immediate improvement to your style.

Here is a selection of alternatives to **dire** and **rispondere**. The past historic of irregular verbs is given in brackets. Try and include as many of them as you can in your active vocabulary:

affermare to state	**notare** to notice
aggiungere (aggiunsi) to add	**obiettare** to object
ammettere (ammisi) to admit	**osservare** to observe
annunciare to announce	**precisare** to clarify
assicurare to assure	**proseguire** to go on
constatare to note	**replicare** to reply
continuare to go on	**ribattere** to retort
dichiarare to declare	**riconoscere (riconobbi)** to admit
domandare to ask	**rivelare** to reveal
esporre (esposi) to outline	**segnalare** to point out
far notare (feci notare) to point out	**sostenere (sostenni)** to maintain, claim
indicare to point out	**sottolineare** to underline
interrompere (interruppi) to interrupt	**spiegare** to explain

These verbs can be used as alternatives to **pensare**:

considerare to consider	**giudicare** to judge
credere to believe	**ritenere (ritenni)** to think
essere (fui) dell'avviso che to be of the opinion that	**trovare** to find

Finally, these verbs indicate different ways of talking:

balbettare to stammer	**mormorare** to murmur
brontolare to grumble	**ruggire** to roar
esclamare to exclaim	**strillare** to shriek
gemere to whine, moan, groan	**sussurrare** to whisper
gridare to shout	**urlare** to scream

Complete the following sentences with an appropriate verb, without using **dire**, **rispondere**, or **pensare**:

1 La maggior parte dei deputati .... che queste misure siano inadeguate.
Most MPs think that these measures are inadequate.

2 Mio marito ed io .... che c'è stato un equivoco.
My husband and I have pointed out that there has been a misunderstanding.

3 Molti studenti .... di non aver letto il libro.
A lot of students have admitted that they have not read the book.

4 Il governo .... che il referendum sarebbe stato rimandato.
The government announced that the referendum would be postponed.

5 Prima di concludere, ... che non c'era altra scelta.
Before concluding, he had added that there was no alternative.

6 Il ministro .... il motivo delle sue dimissioni.
The minister explained the reason for his resignation.

7 .... che se n'erano andati senza fiatare.
He noted that they had left without uttering a word.

8 – Un ragno! – .... la bambina.
'A spider!', shrieked the little girl.

9 – Mi hai salvato la vita: non so come ringraziarti – .... pieno di riconoscenza.
'You have saved my life: I don't know how to thank you', I stammered, full of gratitude.

10 – **Non permetterti di parlarmi con questo tono! –** .... **il padre.**
'Don't you dare speak to me like that!' roared her father.

11 – **Ti parlo come mi pare e piace! –** .... **la figlia.**
'I'll speak to you as I jolly well please!' the daughter snapped back.

12 – **Non ne posso più ... –** .... **il vecchio.**
'I can't take any more ... ' moaned the old man.

II   Stylish alternatives to adverbs

In English, adverbs are frequently added to verbs to describe, for instance, a person's manner of speaking: 'he replied sadly, crossly'. In cases like these, Italian does not use adverbs very often. Fortunately, the alternatives are both easy to use and very stylish. Using them instead of adverbs will make your Italian more idiomatic and more sophisticated. Here are your options:

- Use a noun phrase. For example: **con tristezza** sadly, **con un sorriso** smilingly, **con rabbia** angrily, **con curiosità** inquiringly, **con affetto** affectionately, **con allegria** cheerfully; **senza distinzione** indiscriminately, **senza interruzione** uninterruptedly.
- Use a gerund. For example: **sorridendo** smilingly, **ridendo** laughingly, **tremando** tremulously, **scherzando** jokingly, **facendo una smorfia** with a grimace.
- Use an adjective, making the necessary agreement. For example: **l'insegnante rispose severo/triste/incredulo/distratto** [the teacher replied strictly/sadly/incredulously/absent-mindedly].
- Use one of the following expressions followed by a suitable adjective: **con voce, con aria, con fare, con atteggiamento, con occhi, con lo sguardo**. Here are some examples:

Parlava con voce rauca/melliflua/rotta dalla commozione.
[He spoke hoarsely/sweetly/emotionally]
Si muoveva con aria spavalda/divertita/pensierosa.
[He moved cockily/cheerily/pensively.]
Si rivolse a loro con fare/con atteggiamento aggressivo/disperato.
[He turned to them aggressively/desperately.]
Lo guardava con occhi curiosi/pieni di lacrime.
[She looked at him inquiringly/weepily.]
Lo fissava con lo sguardo assente/perso.
[She stared at him vacantly.]

Complete the sentences with the most suitable expression, using one of the following adjectives: **sarcastico**, **risentito**, **tremante**, **appassionato**, **desolato**.

> **13** – Ma perché tocca sempre a me lavare i piatti? – esclamò Piero ....
> 'Why is it always my turn to wash up?' exclaimed Piero resentfully.
>
> **14** – Non oso dirti la verità ... – confessò ....
> 'I daren't tell you the truth...' she confessed shakily.
>
> **15** – Pensavo che mi aveste abbandonata ... – mormorava la bambina ....
> 'I thought you had abandoned me ...' the little girl whispered, looking distressed.
>
> **16** – Ti voglio davvero tanto bene ... – dichiarò Linda ....
> 'I really love you ...', declared Linda passionately.
>
> **17** – Così sei senza soldi un'altra volta: figuriamoci! – brontolò il padre ....
> 'So you've run out of money once again: I might have known!' grumbled his father sarcastically.

Here are a few more useful idiomatic adverbial expressions for you to learn:

grosso modo broadly, roughly	**per caso** accidentally
prima o poi sooner or later	**per fortuna** luckily
a poco a poco gradually	**per disgrazia** unfortunately
a ragione/a torto rightly/wrongly	**per sbaglio** by mistake
del tutto completely	**in effetti** actually
volentieri willingly	**in fretta** quickly, in a hurry
una volta per tutte once and for all	**in particolare** particularly
tra l'altro incidentally	**ogni tanto** once in a while

III Use of tenses in reported speech

Remember to pay particular attention to the use of tenses in reported speech when the reporting verb is in the past (imperfect, passato prossimo, past historic, pluperfect). The following changes will take place:

Direct speech	Reported speech
Lei è (present)	**Lei era** (imperfect)
Lei sarà (future)	**Lei sarebbe stata** (compound conditional)
Lei sarà stata (future perfect)	**Lei sarebbe stata** (compound conditional)
Lei è stata (passato prossimo)	**Lei era stata** (pluperfect)
Lei sarebbe (conditional)	**Lei sarebbe stata** (compound conditional)

Look at the following examples and note the change of pronouns as well as the change of tenses:

- **Irma è a Milano. – Lucio ha detto che Irma era a Milano.**
  ['Irma is in Milan.' Lucio said that Irma was in Milan.]
- **Sarò contenta di vedervi – Aveva detto che sarebbe stata contenta di vederci.**
  ['I will be pleased to see you.' She had said she would be pleased to see us.]
- **Sono stata a teatro. – Diceva che era stata a teatro.**
  ['I have been to the theatre.' She was saying she had been to the theatre.]
- **Sarei felice di parlarti. – Disse che sarebbe stata felice di parlarmi.**
  ['I would be pleased to talk to you.' She said she would be pleased to talk to me.]

Rewrite the following sentences as reported speech, making any necessary changes to pronouns as well as to verb tenses. Introduce the speech with the verb indicated. Complete the English translation as well.

---

18 – **Marisa sarà felicissima di sentirvi. –**
Paolo ci aveva assicurato che ....
'Marisa will be really pleased to hear from you.'
Paolo ....

19 – **Lei sarà già partita. –**
Obiettarono che ....
'She will already have left.'
They ....

20 – **È dimagrito molto. –**
Hanno osservato che ....
'He has lost a lot of weight.'
They ....

21 – **Il tasso di disoccupazione dovrebbe abbassarsi notevolmente. –**
Il governo ha affermato che ....
'The unemployment rate should fall considerably.'
The government ....

22 – **Non ti sopporto più! –**
Aveva urlato che ....
'I can't stand you any more!'
She ....

23 – Non avrò tempo di leggere l'articolo. –
Aveva precisato che ....
'I won't have time to read the article.'
He ....

IV Use of the conditional for unconfirmed reports

The conditional is often used in the media to relate unconfirmed reports or allegations. For example:

> **Più di cento auto sarebbero coinvolte nel tamponamento a catena.**
> [More than a hundred cars are said to be involved in the pile-up.]
> **I recenti disordini sarebbero stati provocati dagli ultrà romanisti.**
> [The recent riots were allegedly caused by fanatical Rome supporters.]

As you can see from these examples, the simple conditional is used where a present tense would be used in a straightforward statement of fact, while the compound conditional is used instead of a past tense. You can imitate this usage yourself if you are reporting a statement or an allegation which is not your own. It is often useful to introduce such statements with **secondo** 'according to'. Here are some more examples:

> **Secondo gli inquirenti, si tratterebbe di un incendio doloso.**
> [According to the investigating officials, it is a case of arson.]
> **Secondo fonti ufficiose, il primo ministro si sarebbe già dimesso.**
> [According to unofficial sources, the Prime Minister has already resigned.]

Rewrite the following sentences, introducing the statements as indicated, and making clear by your choice of tenses that you do not personally vouch for the truth of what is said:

24 È malato da tre giorni. (Secondo la segretaria, ...)
He has been ill for three days. (According to his secretary, ...)
....

25 Roma è stata fondata da due gemelli, Romolo e Remo. (Secondo la leggenda, ...)
Rome was founded by twin brothers, Romulus and Remus. (According to the legend, ...)
....

26 I capi di stato si erano incontrati segretamente per discutere la crisi. (Secondo fonti autorevoli, ...)

The heads of state had met secretly to discuss the crisis. (According to reliable sources, ...)

....

27 Molti sportivi fanno regolarmente uso di sostanze anabolizzanti. (Secondo le autorità sportive, ...)

Many athletes regularly use anabolic steroids. (According to the sports authorities, ...)

....

28 L'imputato ha rubato quadri e gioielli al fratello. (Secondo i testimoni, ...)

The accused stole pictures and jewellery from his brother. (According to the witnesses, ...)

....

V   Inversion of subject and verb after direct speech

Finally, remember that following a passage of direct speech, you need to place the subject after the verb of saying. For example:

- **Non ho la più pallida idea di dove siano i tuoi occhiali! – rispose la mamma.**
  ['I haven't got the faintest idea where your glasses are!' his mum replied.]
- **Troverete la banca subito a destra, dopo il supermercato. – suggerì il passante.**
  ['You'll find the bank immediately on the right, after the supermarket,' the passer-by suggested.]

Now, make the sentences in the box into direct speech paying particular attention to tense changes, pronouns and inversion of subject and verb, as in the following example:

Gli intervistati sostenevano che i giornalisti facevano loro domande troppo personali.
[The interviewees claimed that the journalists were asking them too personal questions.]

- **I giornalisti ci fanno domande troppo personali – sostenevano gli intervistati.**
  'The journalists ask us too personal questions,' claimed the interviewees.

29 **Sofia aveva ammesso che non sarebbe partita fino a lunedì.**
Sophie had admitted that she would not leave until Monday.

....

30 **La nostra vicina ci domandò se potevamo darle una mano.**
Our neighbour asked us if we could give her a hand.

....

See for further information
Soluzioni!, Chapter 4
A Reference Grammar of Modern Italian, Chapter 13

Key points: Modal verbs

*Do you have problems deciding how to translate the English 'can', 'could', 'may', 'might', 'must', 'ought to', 'should', 'should have', 'will' and 'would' into Italian? Often it is just a matter of choosing the correct tense of **potere**, **dovere** and **volere**, but sometimes this won't do. The exercises in this chapter will help you get your modal verbs right every time.*

I **'Can'/'can't'**

- If 'can' expresses possibility/permission or is used in polite requests, use the present indicative of **potere**. For example:

   Questo può essere un errore.
   [This can be a mistake.]
   Domani non posso uscire.
   [I cannot go out tomorrow.]
   Puoi telefonarmi più tardi?
   [Can you 'phone me later?]
   Scusa, non posso giocare a carte/a tennis.
   [Sorry, I can't (i.e. I'm not allowed to) play cards/tennis.]

- If 'can' expresses ability (to manage to, to be in a position to), use the present indicative of **riuscire a** or **essere in grado di**. If it means 'to know how to', i.e. it expresses an ability acquired through learning how to do something, use the present indicative of **sapere**. For example:

   Paola non riesce ad accendere lo stereo. Aiutala!
   [Paola cannot (i.e. can't figure out how to) turn the hi-fi on. Help her!]
   Non riusciamo a sollevare questa cassa, è troppo pesante.
   [We cannot lift this crate, it's too heavy.]
   Sei in grado di pagare queste rate?
   [Can you pay these instalments?]
   Quante lingue sanno parlare?
   [How many languages can they speak?]
   Scusa, non so giocare a carte/a tennis.
   [Sorry, I can't (i.e. I don't know how to) play cards/tennis.]

- If 'can' is used with a verb of perception, e.g. 'to hear', 'to see', 'to smell', 'to taste', just use the present indicative of the verb of perception. When 'can/can't hear' and 'can/can't see' mean 'to have good/bad hearing' or 'sight', use **sentirci** and **vederci**. For example:

Mi senti, Anna?
[Can you hear me, Anna?]
Non ci vedo niente con questa nebbia.
[I can't see anything in this fog.]
Parla più forte, non ci sento bene.
[Speak up, I can't hear very well.]
Sentite il gusto/il profumo della cannella?
[Can you taste/smell the cinnamon?]

II   'Could'/'couldn't'

- If 'could' expresses possibility or is used in polite requests, use the simple conditional of **potere**. For example:

Questo potrebbe essere un errore.
[This could be a mistake.]
Potresti telefonarmi più tardi?
[Could you 'phone me later?]

- If 'could' expresses ability (to manage to, to be in a position to), use the **passato prossimo** or the imperfect of **riuscire a** or **essere in grado di**, depending on the context. If it means 'to know how to', i.e. it expresses an ability acquired through learning how to do something, use the imperfect or the **passato prossimo** of **sapere**. For example:

Paola non riusciva ad accendere lo stereo.
[Paola couldn't (i.e. couldn't figure out how to) turn the hi-fi on.]
Non siamo riusciti a sollevare questa cassa, era troppo pesante.
[We couldn't lift this crate, it was too heavy.]
Saresti in grado di pagare queste rate?
[Could you pay these instalments?]
Quante lingue sapevano parlare?
[How many languages could they speak?]
Scusa, non ho saputo montare lo scaffale.
[Sorry, I couldn't (i.e. I didn't know how to) put up the shelf.]

- If 'could' is used with a verb of perception, e.g. 'to hear', 'to see', 'to smell', 'to taste', just use the imperfect of the verb of perception. When 'could/couldn't hear' and 'could/couldn't see' mean 'to have good/bad hearing or sight', use **sentirci** and **vederci**. For example:

Mi sentivi, Anna?
[Could you hear me, Anna?]
Non ci vedevo niente con quella nebbia.
[I couldn't see anything in that fog.]

Ha parlato più forte perché non ci sentivo bene.
[S/he spoke up, because I couldn't hear very well.]
Sentivate il gusto/il profumo della cannella?
[Could you taste/smell the cinnamon?]

- If 'could' means 'would be able to', use the simple conditional of **potere**, **riuscire a**, **essere in grado di**, or **sapere**, depending on context. For example:

Potrebbe/riuscirebbe a finire se si sforzasse.
[S/he could (would be able to) finish if s/he made an effort.]
Sarebbero in grado di pagare queste rate se non sprecassero i soldi.
[They could pay these instalments if they didn't waste their money.]
Saprebbe giocare meglio se volesse.
[He could play better if he wanted to.]

Complete the following sentences with the appropriate Italian equivalent of 'can/can't', 'could/couldn't':

---

1 .... *lasciare un messaggio?*
Could I leave a message?

2 *Non .... arrivare in tempo.*
He couldn't (was not able to) arrive on time.

3 *A tre anni .... già leggere.*
At the age of three he could already read.

4 .... *vederci giovedì prossimo, se per te va bene.*
We can meet next Thursday, if that's OK by you.

5 .... *vederci giovedì prossimo, se per te andasse bene.*
We could meet next Thursday, if it were OK by you.

6 *Perchè non .... uscire?*
Why can't I go out?

7 *Sono troppo giovani, non .... capire certe scelte.*
They are too young, they cannot understand certain choices.

8 *Ho le dita troppo grosse, non .... infilare l'ago.*
My fingers are too big, I cannot thread the needle.

III   'May'/'might'

- If 'may' or 'might' express permission or possibility, use the present indicative or the conditional of **potere**. In the case of possibility, you could also use **può darsi che** + subjunctive, the future of the main verb, as seen in Day 13, or simply the adverb **forse** with an appropriate tense of the main verb. For example:

Puoi uscire stasera.
[You may go out this evening.]
Può/potrebbe capitare a tutti.
[It may/might happen to anyone.]
Avresti anche potuto aiutarmi!
[You might have helped me!]
Può darsi che piova./Forse pioverà.
[It may/might rain.]
Può darsi che Ivan sia già arrivato.
[Ivan may/might have arrived already.]
Emanuela non c'è ancora: avrà molto lavoro/avrà trovato traffico per strada.
[Emanuela is not here yet: she may have a lot of work/she may have run into bad traffic on the road.]

- If 'may' or 'might' are in a subordinate clause introduced by a conjunction like 'although' or 'whatever' or after verbs of hoping or fearing, use the required tense of the main verb. For example:

Sebbene sia malato/Anche se è malato, continua a lavorare.
[Although he may/might be ill, he continues to work.]
Ho paura che si faccia male.
[I'm afraid s/he may/might hurt herself/himself.]
Qualsiasi cosa tu dica, non cambierò idea.
[Whatever you may/might say, I won't change my mind.]
Sebbene fosse malato/Anche se era malato, continuava a lavorare.
[Although he may have been ill, he continued to work.]
Avevo paura che si facesse male.
[I was afraid s/he might hurt herself/himself.]

Note the following idiomatic expressions:

     Tanto vale 'may/might as well', as in:
     Ho bisogno di una cartella nuova, tanto vale comprare/ che compri questa.
     [I need a new satchel, I may/might as well buy this one.]
     Avrei dovuto immaginarlo!
     [I might have guessed/known!]

Complete the following sentences with the appropriate Italian equivalent of 'may/might':

---

9 .... *fare come volete.*
You may do as you wish.

10 *Qualsiasi cosa ...., te lo farò sapere.* **(accadere)**
Come what may (whatever may happen), I'll let you know.

11 *Questo .... essere difficile.*
This might be difficult.

12 *Hanno legato il cane per paura che .... * **(scappare)**
They tied the dog up for fear that it might run away.

13 .... *dirmelo prima!*
You might have told me before!

14 *Spero che .... trovare il lavoro che cerca.*
I hope he may succeed in finding the job he's looking for.

15 *Daniele non risponde: ....*
Daniele is not answering: he may have gone out already.

IV 'Must'/'should'/'ought to'

The idea of compulsion or obligation expressed by 'must', 'have to', 'should' and 'ought to' is usually rendered by the appropriate tense of **dovere**, as in:

> **È tardi, devo andare.**
> [It's late, I must go.]
> **Ho dovuto studiare tutto il pomeriggio.**
> [I've had to work all afternoon.]
> **Dovresti fare più sport.**
> [You should (ought to) do more sport.]
> **Avresti dovuto avvertirmi.**
> [You should (ought to) have let me know.]

Remember that 'should have' and 'ought to have' + past participle are translated by the compound conditional of **dovere** + the infinitive of the main verb:

> **Avremmo dovuto telefonare.**
> [We should (ought to) have 'phoned.]

Sometimes 'should' and 'should have' are used instead of 'would' and 'would have', without any idea of obligation, as in:

[I should (= would) like to say ….]
[If I had the time, I should (= would) go to the museum.]
[If I had had the time, I should have (= would have) gone to the museum.]

In cases like these, use the simple and the compound conditional of the main verb respectively:

Vorrei dire …
Se avessi tempo, andrei al museo.
Se avessi avuto tempo, sarei andato al museo.

Finally, occasionally 'should' is the equivalent of a present tense, as in:

Se lo vedi, salutalo da parte mia.
[Should you see him, give him my regards.]

Complete the following sentences with the appropriate Italian equivalent of 'must', 'should', 'ought to':

---

16 *Che cosa* .... *fare?*
What should I do?

17 *Se* ...., *digli che li richiamerò più tardi.*
Should they ring, tell them I'll call them back later.

18 *Non so se* .... *parlarne con Giacomo.*
I don't know whether I should speak to Giacomo about it.

19 *A quanti anni si* .... *andare in pensione, secondo te?*
At what age should one retire, in your opinion?

20 *Se vincessi al lotto,* .... *subito in pensione!*
If I won the lottery, I should retire immediately!

21 *Come vedi,* .... *farlo.*
As you can see, I had to do it.

V   'Will' and 'would'

'Will' usually refers to future events, so the Italian equivalent is the future tense of the main verb, as in:

Usciremo fra poco.
[We will go out in a little while.]

Vi farete male se non fate attenzione.
[You will hurt yourselves if you are not careful.]

If 'will' expresses an idea of wanting or wishing, use an appropriate tense of **volere**. For example:

Fa' come vuoi.
[Do as you will.]
Vuoi una fetta di torta?
[Will you have a slice of cake?]
Proprio non vuoi capire come devi comportarti!
[You just won't understand how you must behave!]

'Would' is mostly a conditional form, so the Italian equivalent is the conditional of the main verb, as in:

Uscirei con voi se avessi tempo.
[I would go out with you if I had time.]
Sarei uscita anch'io se avessi avuto tempo.
[I would have gone out too if I had had time.]

If 'would' expresses an idea of wanting or not wanting to do something, use an appropriate tense of **volere**. For example:

Volete qualcosa da mangiare?
[Would you like something to eat?]
Non ha voluto aiutarmi.
[He would not (= was not willing/refused to) help me.]
Non voleva sentir ragione.
[S/he just wouldn't listen.]

Sometimes 'would' is the equivalent of 'used to' and refers to a habitual action in the past. In this case, use the imperfect indicative in Italian. For example:

Da bambini, andavamo spesso dalla nonna in campagna.
[As children we would often go to our Gran's in the country.]

Complete the following sentences with the appropriate Italian equivalent of 'will' and 'would':

22 .... in Italia se potessi.
I would go to Italy if I could.

23 Patrizia non .... saperne di mettere in ordine la sua camera.
Patrizia won't hear of tidying up her room.

24 La vecchietta .... ore ed ore affacciata alla finestra.
The old lady would spend hours at the window.

25 **I bambini .... con noi stasera.**
The children will stay with us tonight.

26 **Non .... far nulla per aiutarli.**
He wouldn't do anything to help them.

27 **Mi .... una mano?**
Would you give me a hand?

28 **Al posto tuo, non .... così.**
In your shoes, I would not have replied like that.

29 **A quest'ora, ... di parlare col medico.**
By now he will have finished talking to the doctor.

30 **Non .... sedervi cinque minuti?**
Won't you sit down for five minutes?

See for further information
Soluzioni!, pages 209, 216–17, 227, 237–40, 272, 285–8
A Reference Grammar of Modern Italian, Chapter 15

Upgrade your vocabulary: Health

This is another obviously useful topic to be familiar with. Additionally, health is another area of debate which, like education, is on the political agenda and is a key social issue both in the English-speaking world and in Italy. A good command of the vocabulary related to health will give you access to many features and debates in the press and other mass media.

---

stare/sentirsi bene/male to be/feel well/poorly
aver mal di testa/denti/stomaco/orecchi/pancia/schiena to have
   a head/tooth/stomach/ear/tummy/back ache
farsi male to hurt oneself as in **Mi sono fatto male al braccio**
   I have hurt my arm
fare male to hurt as in **Ti fa male la gamba?** Does your leg hurt?

freddo cold
prendere freddo to catch a chill
il raffreddore a cold
prendere/avere il raffreddore to catch/have a cold
il raffreddore da fieno hay fever
sudare freddo to come out in a cold sweat

la febbre fever, temperature
avere la febbre to have a temperature
febbricitante feverish

l'influenza the 'flu
avere l'influenza to have the 'flu

i brividi the shivers
avere i brividi/rabbrividire to shiver

---

1 If a medicine is prescribed for *sintomi influenzali*, what is it for?

....

l'allergia allergy

> **2** Guess 'allergic', as in 'an allergic reaction':
> **una reazione** __ __ __ __ __ __ __ __ __

la salute health
avere una salute di ferro to have an iron constitution
Salute! Cheers!
salutare to greet, say hallo/goodbye
il saluto greeting
sano healthy
l'assistenza sanitaria health care

> **3** Guess 'National Health Service':
> **il** __ __ __ __ __ __ __ __ __   __ __ __ __ __ __ __ __ __ __
> __ __ __ __ __ __ __ __ __

la sindrome syndrome
l'AIDS AIDS
essere sieropositivo/-a to be HIV positive
il/la sieropositivo/-a HIV positive person

l'esaurimento nervoso nervous breakdown
lo stress stress
stressante stressful
lo svenimento fainting fit
svenire to faint

> **4** Guess 'HIV positive status':
> **la** __ __ __ __ __ __ __ __ __ __ __ __ __ __ __ __ __ __ __
> **5** Guess 'exhausted, run down, worn out': __ __ __ __ __ __ __ __ __ __/__

il cancro cancer
cancerogeno carcinogenic
il tumore tumour
la chirurgia surgery (the discipline, not the doctor's consulting room)
l'intervento chirurgico operation
il chirurgo surgeon
la sala operatoria operating theatre
l'ambulatorio doctor's surgery

6 Guess the meaning of **la chirurgia estetica:**

....

7 Guess the meaning of **subire un intervento difficile:**

....

il vaccino vaccine
vaccinare to vaccinate

l'anestesia anaesthetic

8 Guess 'vaccination':

_ _   _ _ _ _ _ _ _ _ _ _ _ _ _

9 Guess 'anaesthetist':

_ _   _ _ _ _ _ _ _ _ _ _ _

10 Guess 'anaesthetize':

_ _ _ _ _ _ _ _ _ _ _ _ _

Now complete the following sentences with the missing words:

11 Perché non _ _ _   _ _ _ _ _ _ _ _ Carlo? – Non l'avevo visto.
Why did you not say hallo to Carlo? – I hadn't noticed him.

12 Molti coloranti alimentari sono stati proibiti perché hanno proprietà

_ _ _ _ _ _ _ _ _ _ _.
Many food colourings have been banned because they have carcinogenic properties.

13 Siete stati _ _ _ _ _ _ _ _ _ _ contro la tubercolosi?
Have you been vaccinated against TB?

14 L'_ _ _ _ _ _ _ _ _ _ _ del Dottor Ferraris è aperto per le visite ai pazienti dalle 2 alle 4.
Dr Ferraris' surgery is open to patients from 2 to 4.

15 - **16** Hai anche tu il _ _ _ _ _ _ _ _ _ _ _ _ _ _ _ _ _ _ ? – No, ma _ _ _ _

_ _ _ _ _ _ _ _ _ ai peli dei gatti.
Do you have hay fever, too? – No, but I am allergic to cats' hair.

17 Quando l'ho visto estrarre la pistola, _ _ _ _ _ _ _ _ _ _ _ _ _ dalla paura.
When I saw him pull out the gun, I came out in a cold sweat with fear.

18 – 19 __ _____ ____ **Laura? Ha l'aria strana. – Non so, forse ha un po'**
d'_____.

*Is Laura feeling all right? She looks strange. – I don't know,
maybe she has a touch of 'flu.*

l'infermiere/-a nurse
il paramedico paramedic

**il medico/il dottore/
la dottoressa** doctor
medico (adj.) medical, as in **assistenza
medica** medical care, **ricetta
medica** prescription and **visita
medica** medical (examination)

la malattia illness
ammalarsi to become ill
la cura cure
curare to cure
essere ricoverato/-a to be in hospital
(NB false friend, *not* 'to recover')
guarire to recover
essere dimesso to be discharged from hospital

gli orecchioni mumps
il morbillo measles

la varicella chicken pox
la rosolia German measles, rubella

l'emicrania migraine
lo sfogo/l'orticaria rash
l'infarto heart attack
l'ictus stroke
i polmoni lungs

la ferita wound
ferire to wound
medicare una ferita to dress a wound
fasciare una ferita to bandage a
    wound

20 Guess the meaning of **la polmonite:**
....

As with English '-itis', **-ite** is a suffix that can be added on to numerous words
to mean an illness related to that noun. In Italian these words are all feminine. Guess the following:

i bronchi bronchial tubes

21 'bronchitis': __ __ _____

22 'arthritis': __ _____

23 'ear infection': __ ' **ot** __ __ __

le tonsille tonsils

24 'tonsillitis': __ __ __ __ __ __ __ __ __ __ __ __

l'appendice appendix

25 'appendicitis': __ ' __ __ __ __ __ __ __ __ __ __ __ __

WORDSEARCH

Find ten of today's words written either horizontally (left to right only) or vertically (downwards only), in the following grid. When you have found them, copy them into the alphabetical list underneath, along with their English translation. Don't forget to include articles with nouns.

```
U  K  H  T  D  F  B  N  S  A  L  U  T  E  N  H  F  V
N  G  H  F  E  R  D  V  I  L  O  H  T  F  E  D  G  C
K  H  T  R  F  D  S  V  E  D  V  U  K  G  V  R  F  A
L  J  M  B  N  F  X  B  R  I  C  E  T  T  A  G  F  S
G  R  F  F  T  S  E  N  O  P  H  B  C  R  R  O  S  F
U  G  P  E  L  T  F  M  P  K  G  T  B  L  I  D  Z  O
L  G  D  B  E  S  A  O  O  E  U  F  R  K  C  S  X  G
T  B  V  B  A  J  H  F  S  V  E  N  I  M  E  N  T  O
L  Z  N  R  K  F  B  U  I  C  I  O  V  L  L  T  P  R
S  T  R  E  S  S  A  N  T  E  L  M  I  F  L  G  X  R
L  H  B  N  F  T  U  S  I  D  Y  O  D  K  A  S  R  O
H  F  B  M  V  S  U  O  V  I  A  P  I  Z  V  X  N  H
K  F  I  N  F  A  R  T  O  P  R  T  K  D  Z  I  A  M
```

1 __ __ __ __ __ __ __
....

6 __ __ __ __ __ __ __
....

2 __ __ __ __ __ __ __ __
....

7 __ __ __ __ __ __ __ __ __ __ __ __
....

3 __ __ __ __ __ __ __ __
....

8 __ __ __ __ __ __ __ __ __ __
....

4 __ __ __ __ __ __ __ __ __
....

9 __ __ __ __ __ __ __ __ __ __ __ __
....

5 __ __ __ __ __ __ __ __
....

10 __ __ __ __ __ __ __ __ __ __ __ __
....

Check your answers against the answer section, then award yourself half a point for each correct answer, for a maximum total of five points.

Key points:
Using possessives correctly

DAY 27

Do you make mistakes with possessives? Are you unsure whether you need an article or not when using possessives with certain words? The following exercises will help you get your possessives correct every time.

I 'His', 'her', 'its', 'their', 'your'
As a general rule, possessive adjectives are used with the definite article and precede the noun they modify. They agree in number and gender with this noun, *not* with the possessor. So, **il suo** and **la sua** can express 'his', 'her', 'its' or the formal 'your' when the object owned is singular and there is one owner, male or female. **I suoi** and **le sue** also mean 'his', 'her', 'its' or the formal 'your', but they refer to plural objects owned and one owner. They *never* mean their.

Il/la/i/le loro mean 'their' and can indicate one or more objects owned, but always more than one owner.

Here are some examples:

> **Silvia non vuole prestarci la sua macchina/il suo motorino/ i suoi appunti/le sue cassette.**
> [Silvia doesn't want to lend us her car/her moped/her notes/her tapes.]
> **Silvio non vuole prestarci la sua macchina/il suo motorino/ i suoi appunti/le sue cassette.**
> [Silvio doesn't want to lend us his car/his moped/his notes/his tapes.]
> **Signor Sarti, ecco il Suo passaporto/la Sua carta d'identità/ i Suoi documenti/le Sue fatture.**
> [Mr Sarti, here is/are your passport/your ID card/your papers/your invoices.]
> **Sandra e Silvio hanno venduto il loro appartamento/la loro casa al mare/i loro mobili antichi/le loro litografie.**
> [Sandra and Silvio have sold their flat/their house at the seaside/ their antique furniture/their lithographs.]

In the following sentences, replace the underlined words with the correct form of **suo** or **loro**, as in the example:

Ex. La macchina <u>di Paola</u> è guasta. La sua macchina è guasta.
Paola's car is faulty.

1 Hai visto l'appartamento nuovo <u>di Riccardo?</u>
Have you seen Richard's new flat?

2 Ti piacciono gli amici <u>di Roberta?</u>
Do you like Roberta's friends?

3 Ti piacciono le amiche <u>di Roberta?</u>
Do you like Roberta's friends?

4 I bambini <u>dei nostri vicini</u> sono molto vivaci.
Our neighbours' children are very lively.

5 La popolazione <u>di Firenze</u> è diminuita.
The population of Florence has gone down.

6 Le piante <u>dei nostri vicini</u> sono davvero rigogliose.
Our neighbours' plants are really luxuriant.

7 L'appartamento <u>dei miei vicini</u> è in vendita.
My neighbours' flat is up for sale.

II   Possessives with words indicating family relationship

With words that indicate family relationship (e.g. **padre**, **madre**, **moglie**, **marito**, **figlio**, **figlia**, **fratello**, **sorella**, **zio**, **zia**, **cugino**, **cugina** etc.), *in their singular form only*, no article is required unless the word is modified by a suffix or prefix, or is accompanied by an adjective. This applies to all possessives except **loro**, which is always preceded by the article. For example:

mio padre my father	**la sua ex-moglie** his ex-wife
sua moglie his wife	**la tua sorella maggiore** your
tua sorella your sister	elder/eldest sister
nostro figlio our son	**il nostro figliolo** our little boy
mio nonno my grandfather	**il mio bisnonno** my great-grandfather
il mio patrigno my stepfather	

sua madre his/her mother   **la sua mamma** his/her mummy
                                   (**mamma**, **papà** and **babbo**
                                   are diminutives)

il loro zio their uncle (**loro** is always preceded by the article)
le mie sorelle my sisters (plurals are always preceded by the article)
il mio bambino my child (**bambino** does not indicate family
   relationship)

Learn the following idiomatic expressions:

a casa mia/tua/sua … in/to   **a modo mio/tuo** …
   my/your/his … house   my/your … way
colpa mia/tua/sua …   **di testa mia/tua** …
   my/your/his … fault   my/your … way
affari miei/tuoi … my/your …   **compito mio/tuo** …
   business   my/your … job
a mia/tua … **disposizione** at   **i miei/tuoi/suoi**
   my/your … disposal   my/your/his/her parents, folks
in camera mia/tua … in   **al posto mio/tuo** …
   my/your … bedroom   in my/your shoes …

In the following sentences, choose the correct form of the possessive:

8 - 10 Ernesto, ti presento (mio/il mio) fratello Giorgio, (mia/la mia) sorellina
Gigliola e (i miei/miei) nonni materni.
*Ernesto, can I introduce my brother George, my little sister
Gigliola and my maternal grandparents?*

11 - 12 Questa è (mia/la mia) seconda moglie Paola e queste sono (le nostre/
nostre) figlie gemelle, Anna e Cristina.
*This is my second wife Paola and these are our twin daughters,
Anna and Cristina.*

13 - 14 Vorrei presentarti (mio/il mio) figlio più grande, Davide, e (la sua/sua)
fidanzata, Alessandra.
I'd like to introduce my eldest son David and his fiancée, Alexandra.

15 Quasi tutte le specie animali proteggono (loro/i loro) piccoli.
Almost all animal species protect their young.

16 - 18 Non preoccuparti, questo ritardo non è (la tua colpa/colpa tua). Appena
arriviamo (alla mia casa/a casa mia) telefoniamo (a tuoi/ ai tuoi).
*Don't worry, this delay is not your fault. As soon as we get to
my house, we'll phone your parents.*

III   Other uses of possessives

As well as with the definite article, possessives can be used with other determining words, such as the indefinite article, numerals, demonstratives and indefinites. Look at the following examples:

> **un mio amico/collega/cliente/parente** a friend/colleague/
>   client/relative of mine
> **due nostri amici/colleghi/conoscenti/compagni di scuola**
>   two friends/colleagues/acquaintances/school friends of ours
> **tre delle mie amiche/sorelle/vicine di casa** three of my
>   friends/sisters/neighbours
> **questa tua decisione** this decision of yours
> **quel suo conoscente** that acquaintance of his
> **qualche mia amica** some friend(s) of mine
> **alcuni loro parenti** some relatives of theirs
> **dei vostri studenti** some students of yours
> **ogni nostro amico** each friend of ours
> **tutti i vostri parenti** all of your relatives

Complete the following sentences with the correct expression:

19 **Marina è** ....
   Marina is a friend of mine.

20 **Alberto è** ....
   Albert is a colleague of his.

21 **Viene alla festa con** ....
   She is coming to the party with four of her (female) cousins.

22 **Abbiamo cenato con** ....
   We had dinner with some clients of ours.

23 **Non capisco** .... **atteggiamento.**
   I don't understand this attitude of yours.

24 .... **proprio non mi piacciono.**
   I really don't like those friends of yours.

25 **Ho riletto** ....
   I reread all of his letters.

IV　When not to use possessives

There are some instances when the possessive in Italian is not required, while it is necessary in the equivalent English sentence. Generally speaking, possessives are not necessary when it is clear from the context who or what belongs to whom, for instance when talking about clothes, personal possessions, parts of the body and sometimes family. Look at the following examples:

Ti sei sporcato i pantaloni.
[You've got your trousers dirty.]
Ho dimenticato l'ombrello a casa tua.
[I left my umbrella at your house.]
Mi dia il passaporto, per favore.
[Can I have your passport, please?]
Non trovo più gli occhiali da sole.
[I can't find my sunglasses any more.]
Maddalena ha gli occhi azzurri e i capelli lunghissimi.
[Maddalena's eyes are blue and her hair is really long.]
La bambina ha battuto la testa.
[The little girl bumped her head.]
Mi fa male la schiena.
[My back aches.]
Prima di andare al lavoro, Anna porta i figli a scuola.
[Before going to work, Anna takes her children to school.]
Telefona pure alla mamma!
[Do 'phone your mum!]

In the following sentences, decide whether the possessive is necessary or not:

---

26 – 27 Mi si è guastato (il computer/il mio computer), ma per fortuna posso usare quello (del fratello/di mio fratello).
My computer is broken, but luckily I can use my brother's.

28 Susanna ha perso (la sua carta/la carta) d'identità.
Susan has lost her ID card.

29 – 30 Se vado ad abitare da solo, chi mi laverà (i miei vestiti/i vestiti), e chi mi farà (la spesa/la mia spesa)?
If I go and live on my own, who will wash my clothes and do my shopping?

See for further information

Soluzioni!, Chapter 8
A Reference Grammar of Modern Italian, Chapter 10

Do you find that you sometimes make mistakes with words that look very similar in English and Italian? Do you sometimes misspell Italian words that are slightly different from their English lookalikes?

The following exercises are designed to help you to become aware of these types of error and to avoid them. Without them, your Italian will be much more accurate and sophisticated.

I Deceptive lookalikes

Note the following **falsi amici** – Italian words which look very similar to English words, but which have a different meaning – and note also the Italian equivalent of the English lookalike. The asterisked items are further illustrated in sample sentences at the end of the list.

Falsi amici	English equivalent	English lookalike	Italian equivalent
annoiare	to bore	to annoy	**seccare, infastidire**
argomento	topic, subject	argument	**litigio, discussione**
assumere	to take on staff	to assume	**supporre, ritenere**
*__attitudine__	aptitude	attitude	**atteggiamento**
carattere	personality	character	**personaggio**
*__confidenza__	familiarity, intimacy	confidence	**fiducia, sicurezza**
consistente	considerable, substantial	consistent	**coerente**
educazione	upbringing	education	**istruzione**
educato	polite	educated	**colto, istruito**
effettivo	actual, real	effective	**efficace**
facilità	ease, ability	facilities	**attrezzature**
finalmente	at last	finally	**infine, per finire**
*__impressionare__	to shock, upset	to impress	**colpire**
libreria	bookshop, bookcase	library	**biblioteca**
parenti (m. pl.)	relatives	parents	**genitori**
*__pretendere__	to expect, to claim	to pretend	**fare finta di**

*realizzare	to make, implement	to realize	rendersi conto di
ricoverare	hospitalize	recover	guarire
ritornare	to come back	to return (give back)	restituire
sensibile	sensitive	sensible	sensato
simpatia	liking, attraction	sympathy	comprensione, compassione
*sopportare	to stand, endure	to support	fare il tifo per, mantenere sostenere, finanziare

attitudine/atteggiamento [talent/attitude]

Tuo fratello ha una spiccata attitudine per le lingue straniere.
[Your brother has a definite talent for foreign languages.]
Non riesci in matematica, non perché non capisci i concetti, ma perché sei prevenuto: hai un atteggiamento troppo negativo.
[You don't do well in maths, not because you don't understand the rules, but because you are prejudiced: your attitude is too negative.]

confidenza/fiducia [closeness/confidence]

Ci conosciamo da molto tempo, ma non abbiamo molta confidenza.
[We have known each other for a long time, but we are not very close.]
Non aveva molta fiducia nelle capacità della sua segretaria.
[S/he did not have much confidence in her/his secretary's ability.]

impressionare/colpire [shock/impress]

Se ti impressiona la vista del sangue, non guardare questo film.
[If the sight of blood shocks you, don't watch this film.]
La bravura degli attori ha colpito tutti.
[The actors' skill impressed everyone.]

pretendere/fare finta di [demand/pretend]

I dipendenti pretendevano un trattamento migliore.
[The employees were demanding better treatment.]
Non far finta di non sapere che tocca a te pagare!
[Don't pretend you don't know it's your turn to pay!]

realizzare/rendersi conto di [make/realize]

Quest'opera d'arte è stata realizzata interamente in vetro.
[This work of art has been made entirely of glass.]
Non si rendono conto della portata delle loro azioni.
[They do not realise the significance of their actions.]

sopportare/fare il tifo per [bear/support]

La tua insolenza è dura da sopportare!
[Your insolence is hard to bear!]
Per quale squadra fai il tifo?
[Which team do you support?]

Now complete the following sentences with the correct word, choosing from the alternatives given in brackets:

---

1 È una persona davvero (educata, colta): sa qualcosa su tutto!
S/he is a really knowledgeable person: s/he knows something about everything!

2 Dopo (una discussione, un argomento) molto acces(a,o), si sono finalmente messi d'accordo.
After a very heated argument, they at last reached agreement.

3 - 4 Non possiamo fare tardi: la (libreria, biblioteca) chiude fra poco e dobbiamo assolutamente (ritornare, restituire) questi libri.
We mustn't be late: the library will close soon and we absolutely must return these books.

5 Le (facilità, attrezzature) sportive della vostra città sono ottime.
The sporting facilities in your town are excellent.

6 Che bambini (educati, colti)! Ma si comportano sempre così bene?
What polite children! But are they always so well behaved?

7 **Secondo voi, quali (caratteri, personaggi) sono poco sviluppati in questo romanzo?**
In your opinion, which characters are not well developed in this novel?

8 **(Supponevo, Assumevo) che sarebbero venuti anche loro.**
I assumed they would come, too.

9 **Rimasero orfani dopo la morte dei (parenti, genitori) in un incidente stradale.**
They were orphaned following their parents' death in a car crash.

10 **Queste compresse per il mal di testa sono davvero (efficaci, effettive).**
These headache tablets are really effective.

11 **È (ricoverata, guarita) tua sorella? Sì, ora sta bene.**
Has your sister recovered? Yes, she's fine, now.

12 **Gli ho spiegato le mie difficoltà, ma non è stato per niente (comprensivo, simpatico).**
I explained my difficulties to him, but he was not at all sympathetic.

13 **Eccoti, (infine, finalmente): ti aspetto da più di mezz'ora.**
Here you are, at last: I've been waiting for you for more than half an hour.

14 **Con il suo comportamento (sensato, sensibile) ha evitato che la situazione diventasse seria.**
With her/his sensible behaviour s/he prevented the situation from becoming serious.

15 **Perché avete l'aria così (annoiata, seccata)? Non avete niente da fare?**
Why are you looking so bored? Don't you have anything to do?

Check that you are really confident by supplying the correct words yourself. In the following sentences, use the English translation to help you fill the gaps:

16 **Il Ministro della Pubblica .... ha intenzione di modificare i programmi di studio della scuola secondaria.**
The Minister for Education intends to modify the syllabus of secondary schools.

17 **Scusami, non .... che fosse già così tardi!**
Sorry, I hadn't realized it was already so late!

18 Questa organizzazione .... interamente da contributi di beneficenza.
This organization is supported entirely by charitable contributions.

19 Che tipo ....!
What a nice chap!

20 – 21 Per essere veramente ...., le riforme economiche devono far parte
di un programma ....
*To be really effective, economic reforms must be part of a
consistent program.*

In sentence 20–21, did you remember that **programma** is masculine?

II   Spelling problems

You have probably already noticed that many Italian words are very similar to
their English equivalent. Words like **elegante, positivo, scientifico, valido,
centrale** and **qualità** are easy to understand and to guess. Following the
same patterns, write the Italian equivalent of the missing words:

22 an alternative choice   *una scelta* ....

23 plastic surgery   *la chirurgia* ....

24 marginal importance   *importanza* ....

25 necessity   ....

In other cases, the Italian equivalent is less close to the English spelling, but
it is still possible to see a pattern. Look at these Italian words and try to work
out the patterns:

**Confusione, decisione, impressione; attivo, attore, perfetto, aspetto;
terribile, probabile, possibile; assurdo, assoluto, osservare; soluzione,
nazione, stazione; famoso, nervoso, misterioso; telefono, fotografia,
elefante.**

Now write the Italian equivalent of the missing words:

26   electricity   ....

27 – 28 a glorious but adventurous past **un passato** .... **ma** ....

29	a nice expression	**una bella** ....
30	An inflexible judge	**un giudice** ....

Finally, remember the following spellings:

responsabile, comunicazione, commedia, drammatico, accademico.

Revision:
Key points

Has the work you have done over the past month to consolidate the key points of the language been effective? Today you can find out how much you have actually assimilated. Before carrying out the revision test, spend at least an hour revising the chapters on key points. Make sure you check your active knowledge (i.e. from English into Italian) as well as your passive (from Italian into English). When you are satisfied that you have revised and checked everything, take a break for at least an hour, then do the revision test below.

Score half a point for each correct (including spelling and accents!) answer. If you manage to score over 20 points out of 30, your accuracy and grammatical competence have increased by two-thirds of what is in this book. If you achieve fewer than 15 points, you need to revise your learning strategies to find the best ones for the way your understanding works (see the Introduction), then go through the chapters on key points again.

Revise Chapters 1, 3, 5, 7 and 9, then complete the following sentences:

1 - **2** Quest_ programma di studi è radical_ e progressist_ e offre ottim_ opportunità di sviluppo.
This curriculum is radical and progressive and offers excellent opportunities for development.

3 Preferirei parlare con .... mi ha scritto la lettera .... ho ricevuto ieri.
I would prefer to speak to the person who sent me the letter that I received yesterday.

4 Per favore, ricordatevi di restituire tutto .... vi è stato prestato dalla scuola.
Please, remember to return everything that has been lent to you by the school.

5 Questo articolo non è tropp_ difficile da capire e sono sicuro che mi servirà molt_.
This article is not too hard to understand and I am sure it will be very useful.

6 Il medico viene tutt_ i pomeriggi, ma il paziente sta decisamente ....
The doctor calls every afternoon, but the patient is definitely better.

7 Il congresso avrà luogo .... due mesi e si terrà ancora .... nella nostra Sede di Milano.
The conference will take place in two months' time and will be held once again in our Milan offices.

8 .... comincerà lo spettacolo.
The show will begin any moment now.

9 .... (interessare) l'arte moderna? – Mi incuriosisce, ma spesso le opere non .... molto.
Are you interested in modern art? – I am curious about it, but often I don't like the works very much.

10 Vi .... (bastare) i soldi che vi ho dato? – Sì, grazie, e il film ci .... molto.
Was the money I gave you enough? – Yes, thanks, and we liked the film a lot.

Revise Chapters 11, 13, 14, 15 and 17, then complete the following sentences:

11 Mentre .... (fare) la spesa, ... (incontrare) il mio insegnante di matematica.
While we were doing the shopping, we bumped into my maths teacher.

12 Quando .... (venire) a trovarci, ... sempre felici di vederli.
When they came to visit us, we were always happy to see them.

13 Giulia .... (cominciare) a studiare il francese quando .... sette anni.
Giulia started learning French when she was seven years old.

14 Chi ha rotto questo bicchiere? – .... Franco, prima .... (lavare) i piatti.
Who broke this glass? It may have been Franco, he was washing up earlier.

15 È deludente che i giovani .... (leggere) così .... libri.
It's disappointing that young people read so few books.

16 Era ora che .... (arrivare)! Vi aspettiamo .... mezz'ora!
It was about time you came! We have been waiting for you for half an hour!

17 A sentire come .... (condurre) la selezione, sono .... veramente amareggiata.
Hearing how the selection had been carried out, I was left very bitter.

18 .... (mandare) un modulo che .... assolutamente compilato entro domani.
I have been sent a form that must without fail be filled in by tomorrow.

19 Dopo .... (scrivere) una lettera ai suoi genitori, è partito.
After writing a letter to his parents, he left.

20 Si arrabbiano sempre .... (parlare) di politica, ma preferiscono .... (discutere) apertamente le cose.
They always get angry when talking about politics, but they prefer to discuss matters openly.

Revise Chapters 19, 21, 23, 25 and 27, then complete the following sentences:

21 Per favore, signora, ... (portare) delle carote.
Please, madam, bring me some carrots.

22 Non .... (fare) stare in pensiero, Roberto, ... (tornare) presto.
Don't make me worry, Roberto, come back early.

23 Entro quando .... (finire) questa relazione?
By when must one finish this report?

24 Quando .... viziat_ come lui, ... (pretendere) sempre molto.
When one is as spoilt as he is, one always expects a lot.

25 Se me lo ...., ti .... aiutata.
If you had asked me, I would have helped you.

26 Se ...., ... al cinema invece che al parco.
Should it rain, we shall go the cinema rather than to the park.

27 Non immaginavo che tu .... sciare così bene.
I never thought you could ski so well.

28 Se te lo ...., ... il mio indirizzo.
Should he ask you for it, give him my address.

29 .... fratello non ha fatto l'università, ma .... sorella minore ha studiato medicina.
My brother never went to university, but my younger sister has studied medicine.

30 Sei un impiccione, fatti ....!
You are a busybody, mind your own business!

Have the vocabulary-learning strategies you have used to memorise the new words and expressions contained in this book been effective? Today you can find out how much you have actually assimilated. Before carrying out the revision test, spend at least an hour revising the chapters on vocabulary and style. Make sure you check your active knowledge (i.e. from English into Italian) as well as your passive (from Italian into English). When you are satisfied that you have revised and checked everything, take a break for at least an hour, then do the revision test below.

Score half a point for each correct (including spelling and accents!) answer. If you manage to score above 20 points out of 30, your active vocabulary has increased by two-thirds of what is in this book. If you achieve fewer than 15 points, you need to revise your learning strategies to find the best ones for the way your memory works (see the Introduction), then go through the vocabulary and style chapters again.

Write down the Italian for the following:

1	cheeky	_ _ _ _ _ _ _ _ _/-a
	nosy parker	**un/-a** _ _ _ _ _ _ _ _ _
2	episode (of a TV serial)	**la** _ _ _ _ _ _ _ _
	horror movie	**un** _ _ _ _ _ _ _ _ _' _ _ _ _ _ _
3	football ground	**lo** _ _ _ _ _ _ _
	to play an instrument	_ _ _ _ _ _ _ _ _ _ _ _ _ _ _ _ _
4	chapter	**il** _ _ _ _ _ _ _ _
	fiction	**la** _ _ _ _ _ _ _ _ _ _
5	to play a part	_ _ _ _ _ _ _ _ _
	picture/painting	**il** _ _ _ _ _ _ _
6	freedom, liberty	_ _ _ _ _ _ _ _ _
	to lose	_ _ _ _ _ _ _
7	Northern	_ _ _ _ _ _ _ _ _ _ _ _ _ _ _
	percentage	**la** _ _ _ _ _ _ _ _ _ _ _

Now give the opposite of the following adjectives:

8 impegnato/-a _____/-a
conformista _____

9 altruista _____
maturo/-a _____/-a

10 ambizioso/-a _____
timido/-a _____/-a

Write down the Italian for the following:

11 additionally _____
mostly ___ __ ___

12 politicians i_____
power il_____

13 middle class la_____
civil rights i_____ _____

14 a brainwave un_____ __ _____
ingenious _____

15 to recycle _____
pollution l'_____

16 school subject la_____
to be a essere_____/-a __ __
graduate in

17 to clarify _____
to whisper _____

18 by mistake ____ _____
gradually a_____ _ _____

19 stressful to recover _____
(from illness) _____

20 educated _____/-a
at last _____

Give two suitable alternatives for the following conjunctions:

21 **perché**
_ _ _ _ _   _ _ _ _
_ _ _   _ _ _ _ _ _   _ _ _ _

22 **ma**
_ _ _   _ _ _ _ _ _
_ _ _ _ _ _ _ _ _

23 **allora**
_ _ _   _ _ _ _ _ _ _ _ _ _ _
_ _ _ _ _ _ _ _ _

Finally, complete the following sentences with the missing words:

24 **Vuoi sempre fare di testa tua: sei davvero** _ _ _ _ _ _ _ _ _ **/-a!**
You always want to do things your way: you are really stubborn!

25 **Non a tutti piace lo stile liberty, è una questione di** _ _ _ _ _ _ **personali.**
Not everybody likes liberty, it's a matter of personal taste.

26 **Quasi tutti i quotidiani italiani contengono ormai uno o più** _ _ _ _ _ _ _ _.
Almost all Italian dailies now contain one or more supplements.

27 **Segue ora un** _ _ _ _ _ _ _ _ _ **dal nostro inviato in Libano.**
We have now a report from our correspondent in Lebanon.

28 **Cerca di leggere Seta, è un** _ _ _ _ _ _ _ _ **davvero fuori del comune.**
Try to read Silk, _it's a novel that is really out of the ordinary._

29 **Se gli agricoltori non ricevessero le** _ _ _ _ _ _ _ _ _ _ _ _ **statali, molti fallirebbero.**
If farmers did not receive state subsidies, many would go out of business.

30 **Negli ultimi anni sono stati fatti grandi** _ _ _ _ _ _ _ _ _ **nella lotta contro il cancro.**
Great progress has been made in recent years in the fight against cancer.

Progress Chart

Use this chart to track your daily progress. Use three colours: one for the vocabulary sections, one for grammar and one for style. That way you will be able to see at a glance if you are weaker in one of the three areas and then make a special effort to compensate for that.

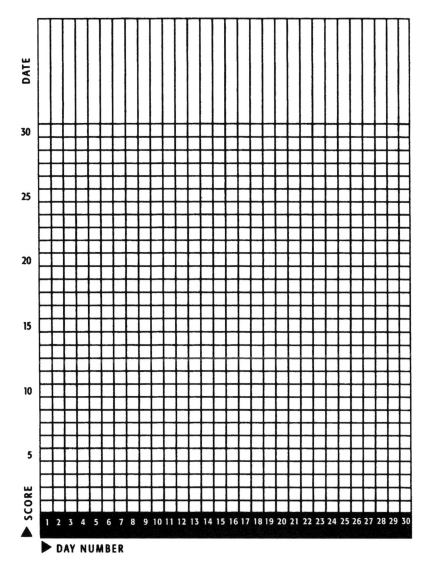

DATE

30

25

20

15

10

5

SCORE

1 2 3 4 5 6 7 8 9 10 11 12 13 14 15 16 17 18 19 20 21 22 23 24 25 26 27 28 29 30

▶ DAY NUMBER

Answers to Exercises

Day 1
AGREEMENT I
1–3 ambientale, serio, difficile
4–5 ultima, bella
6–7 tua, rossa
8 diversa
9–10 realista, complessa
11 notturno
12–13 diritti fondamentali
14–15 leggi fasciste

16–17 spiegazioni insufficienti
18–19 società occidentali
20–21 brutte abitudini
22–23 problemi iniziali
24–25 capaci, violente
26–27 presenti, entusiasti
28 continui
29 utile
30 scritte

Day 2
DESCRIBING PEOPLE
1–3 cortissimi, nera; crew cut and black goatee
4–5 triste; beard
6–8 stanca, scure; tired face, rings under eyes
9 barba
10 sboccato
11 occhiata
12 boccata

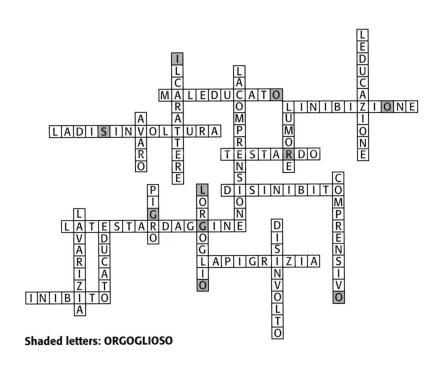

Shaded letters: ORGOGLIOSO

13 l'educazione,
educato,
maleducato
14 la pigrizia, pigro
15 la testardaggine,
testardo
16 l'orgoglio,
orgoglioso
17 l'avarizia, avaro
18 l'inibizione, inibito,
disinibito
19 la disinvoltura,
disinvolto
20 la comprensione,
comprensivo
21 l'umore, il
carattere
22 le cinture di
sicurezza
23–24 giacca,
maniche di camicia
25–26 calze, scalzi
27–28 vestaglia,
camicie da notte
nuove
29–30 borse di
studio, meritevoli

Day 3
RELATIVE PRONOUNS
1 Chi è quel tipo con
gli occhiali?
2 Con chi sei uscita
ieri sera?
3 Per chi compra tutti
quei regali?
4 Quella ragazza coi
capelli lunghi e
biondi che sta
parlando con
Cristiano si chiama
Laura.
5 L'altra sera al
ristorante ho rivisto

un vecchio amico,
Paolo, che avevo
conosciuto quando
abitavo a Padova.
6 A volte è
sconcertante
lavorare con
persone
ambiziosissime, che
pensano
esclusivamente alla
propria carriera.
7 che
8 che
9 chi
10 chi
11 che
12 chi
13 che
14 chi
15 Anche ieri Paolo è
arrivato al lavoro in
ritardo, il che non ha
stupito nessuno.
16 L'Articolo 3 della
Costituzione
sancisce
l'uguaglianza delle
donne agli uomini, il
che può sembrare
strano, considerata
la situazione della
maggioranza delle
donne italiane.
17 Il lavoratore
italiano non può
rinunciare alle ferie,
il che significa che è
obbligato a riposarsi!
18 il che
19 per cui
20 il che
21 per cui
22 per cui

23 Siamo andati a
trovare dei nostri
amici la cui casa si
trova vicino allo
stadio.
24 Sosteniamo che lo
stato debba tutelare
tutte le comunità la
cui lingua è
minoritaria.
25 Silvio si è fidanzato
con una ragazza il
cui padre è
deputato in
parlamento.
26 Non mi piacciono i
ragazzi i cui capelli
sono troppo pieni di
gel.
27 tutto quello/ciò che
28 tutto quello/ciò di
cui
29 Quello/Ciò che
30 quello/ciò che

Day 4
LEISURE, YOUTH
CULTURE AND MUSIC
1 capricious,
whimsical
2 il disaccordo
3 the clash between
generations
4 the sign of
belonging
5 la ribellione
6 to live up to
expectations
7 l'immaginazione
8 immaginare
9 egocentric
10 generoso
11 to speak with
confidence

12 team sport
13 l'allenamento
14 coach
15 the supporters of the English team
16 out of tune
17 armonioso
18 l'armonica a bocca
19 choral music
20 il/la violinista
21 il/la batterista
22 string quintet
23 a hit song
24 la registrazione
25 la composizione
26–27 The disco is the most important meeting place for today's young people. Dancing is the only way to express what you are and what you feel.
28–29 18- to 24-year-olds are today in Italy the keenest cinema-goers, the most assiduous listeners of commercial radio stations, the most regular readers – the women in particular – of magazines.
30 Have you heard this group's latest CD? The singer is brilliant, but the guitarist, the keyboard player and the bass player are also excellent musicians.

Day 5
AGREEMENT II
1–2 [ ] [X]
3–4 [X] [ ]
5–7 [X] [X] [ ]
8–9 [X] [ ]
10–11 molto, pochissimi
12–13 troppi, molto
14–15 poco, parecchi
16–19 molto, tantissimi, troppo, pochi
20 bene, meglio
21 buon, migliore
22 buone, migliore
23 bene, peggio
24 Vieni a trovarmi tutte le volte che vuoi.
25 Qualche volta vado in piscina.
26 Tutte queste tovaglie sono state ricamate.
27 Ogni volta che la vedo ha una pettinatura diversa.
28 Conosci tutti?
29 Ho letto tutti e quattro i suoi libri.
30 Tutte le critiche che hanno ricevuto sono state ingiuste.

Day 6
MASS MEDIA
1 to broadcast
2 il videoregistratore
3 TV game show
4 TV serial
5 presentare
6 TV commercial
7 un programma d'attualità
8 mass culture
9 public opinion
10 la rubrica sportiva
11 women's fashion weekly
12 multiplex, multiscreen
13 sottotitolare
14 to plot
15 a critical and public success
16 l'interpretazione
17 drama school
18 action film
19 epic film
20 musical
21 un film drammatico
22 a weepy
23 cartoons
24–27 Half comic, half tragic; half amusing, half moving: Roberto Benigni's first film with a dramatic element as well is two separate films.The two parts remain separate, the film is not entirely successful but it is the best so far directed by Benigni and he's an excellent hero.
28–30 The language of advertising mustn't just grab the attention, it must also be easy to

remember; in other words, this language must be above all expressive.

Day 7
EXPRESSIONS OF TIME
1 tre volte
2 l'orario
3 tempo
4 in tempo
5 qualche volta
6 il momento
7 Un'altra volta
8 A quei tempi
9 volte
10 tempo
11 ora
12 tempo
13 per
14 da
15 per
16 per
17 da
18 per
19 in
20 fra
21 in
22 Durante
23 di
24 È stata un'annata pessima
25 una giornata
26 sera
27 mattinata
28 serata
29 Ci penso da molto tempo: lo faccio fra un minuto.
30 Ci ho pensato per molto tempo: posso farlo in un minuto.

Day 8
LITERATURE AND VISUAL ARTS
1 literary criticism
2 letteralmente
3 il dialogo
4 il monologo
5 a romantic novel
6 romantico/-a
7 a thriller
8 a love story
9 a sports personality
10 favoloso
11 rimare con
12 onomatopoeia
13 onomatopoeic
14 l'assonanza
15 alliteration
16 ritmico
17 hendecasyllable
18 simbolico, il simbolismo, il/la simbolista
19 Il monologo di Amleto è uno dei brani shakespeariani più famosi.
20 Il Teatro Stabile di Torino metterà in scena 'Il gioco delle parti' di Pirandello.
21 Prima di arrivare al successo, molti comici d'avanguardia recitano sui palcoscenici dei cabaret.
22 fotogenico
23 fotomontaggio
24 brush stroke
25 video library
26 il/la ritrattista
27 l'acquarellista

28 to portray
29 camera
30 oil painting

Day 9
PIACERE AND OTHER IMPERSONAL VERBS
1–2 piace, piace
3 piacciono
4 piace
5 piacciono
6 piacciono
7–8 vi piacerebbe, ci piacciono
9–10 gli piace, gli piacciono
11–12 mi piace, mi piacciono
13 Sì, mi piacerebbe molto.
14 No, non è vero, ci piace.
15 Mi piacciono tutti!
16 È vero, non le piacciono.
17 a noi
18 A lui
19 a loro
20 a me
21 Vi è piaciuta la mia festa?
22 Scusami, i frutti di mare proprio non mi sono piaciuti.
23 A chi non sarebbe piaciuto fare una bella vacanza?
24 Penso che a nessuno sia piaciuto il suo comportamento.
25 Sarà piaciuto alla mamma quel ristorante? E chi lo sa?

26 Ti/Vi basterà una settimana per finire il lavoro?

27 Ci servirà il vocabolario durante l'esame?

28 Gli conviene/converrebbe parlarne con il suo/la sua insegnante.

29 I tuoi/vostri problemi non interessano a nessuno.

30 Se andrai/andrete all'estero, chi ti/vi mancherà di più?

Day 10
DATES AND HISTORY

1 Oggi è lunedì due luglio duemilaquattro.

2 Sono nato/a l'otto giugno millenovecentosettantaquattro, di sabato.

3 Londra, undici maggio millenovecentosessantacinque.

4 Giovedì, venticinque dicembre millesettecentosettantotto.

5 È successo il primo febbraio milleseicentonovantatré.

6 Nel seicentotrentanove avanti Cristo.

7 Enrico VIII (ottavo).

8 Elisabetta II (seconda).

9 Dal millenovecentotrentanove al millenovecentoquarantacinque.

10 Entro il trentun marzo duemilacinque.

11 il/la guerriero/-a
la guerriglia
il/la guerrigliero/-a
Star Wars

12 imperiale
imperare
imperante
imperioso
l'imperatore
l'imperatrice
l'imperialismo

13 l'età dell'oro
l'età del bronzo
l'età della pietra
coetaneo
la terza età
la mezz'età

14 vittorioso
invincibile
il vincitore/
la vincitrice
vincente

15 reale
regnare
regnante
il Regno Unito
la regina

16 la povertà
la nobiltà
la libertà

17 la ricchezza
la forza

18 perdente
la perdita

19 l'antichità
l'antiquariato
l'antiquario

20 il/la servo/-a
la servitù
servizievole
servile

21 la schiavitù

22 l'eroina
l'eroismo
eroico

23 il/la rivoluzionario/-a
controrivoluzionario

24 lottare con
la lotta di classe

25 ribellarsi contro
ribelle
il/la ribelle

26 senza tregua

27 rappacificare
pacifico
il/la pacifista

28 storico
lo/-a storico/-a

29 militarismo
patriottismo
nazionalismo
comunismo

30 fascismo
colonialismo
espansionismo
pacifismo

Day 11
USING THE IMPERFECT CORRECTLY

1 All'incrocio, il vigile dirigeva il traffico.

2 Il bambino piangeva nel suo lettino.

3–4 Il bambino è caduto e ha pianto per dieci minuti.

5 In quel negozio ieri vendevano dei bellissimi oggetti di ceramica.

6 Finalmente Giulia mi ha venduto uno dei suoi quadri.

7–8 Riccardo suonava il suo pezzo preferito al pianoforte e tutti lo ascoltavano senza fiatare.

9 Durante il concerto, il pianista ha suonato tre pezzi di Mozart.

10–11 Suo padre non era vecchio, ma aveva l'aria stanca.

12 Marco ha avuto l'ulcera per molti anni, ma adesso sta bene.

13–14 Non avevano nessun interesse, erano molto pigri.

15–16 Che ora era quando siete arrivati, ragazzi?

17 Siamo stati/e due ore dal dentista!

18 Marina ha sempre avuto i capelli lunghi.

19–20 Marina era molto carina: aveva la frangia e le lentiggini.

21 Dicevo sempre la verità quando ero piccola.

22 Mia madre mi ha sempre detto di non fidarmi dei commercianti.

23 Mamma, quando hai conosciuto papà?

24 Ho saputo che cerchi lavoro, è vero?

25 Pensavamo di mandare una cartolina a Roberto.

26 Abbiamo pensato di mandare una cartolina a Roberto.

27–28 Mentre guidavo, ho guardato per caso nello specchietto: dietro di me c'era una macchina nera che mi seguiva.

29–30 Una mia amica voleva una borsa di pelle per il suo compleanno, così ho girato tutti i negozi del centro per ore ma non sono riuscito/a a trovare la borsa che voleva lei.

Day 12
GEOGRAPHY
1 food chain
2 la reazione a catena
3 mountain climate
4 the Middle-Eastern crisis
5 i Paesi dell'Estremo Oriente
6 the land of the rising sun
7 to promise the earth

8 in riva al mare
9 Il sud-est dell'Inghilterra è la regione più ricca del Paese.

10 È una ditta con succursali in quasi tutti i Paesi dell'Europa occidentale.

11 I popoli dell'Europa meridionale hanno uno stile di vita invidiato dal resto del continente.

12 Parto domani per le vacanze ma ho ancora un mare di lavoro da sbrigare.

13 Mair è di Cardiff. È gallese.

14 La moda parigina mi piace meno di quella milanese.

15–16 Sono nata a Venezia ma i miei sono di Firenze, allora non so se sentirmi veneziana o fiorentina.

17–19 Nelle scuole italiane ci sono sempre più bambini marocchini, polacchi e rumeni.

20–21 Il governo britannico e quello statunitense hanno rapporti di collaborazione molto stretti.

22 family planning
23 urban myth

24 i Paesi in via di sviluppo

25 il piano di sviluppo

26 I bellissimi paesaggi toscani hanno ispirato moltissimi poeti e artisti, sia italiani che stranieri.

27 Alla premiazione, l'orchestra ha suonato la Marsigliese, l'inno nazionale francese.

28–29 Il vero problema non sono gli immigrati con regolare permesso di soggiorno, ma i clandestini.

30 Le statistiche della disoccupazione giovanile in Italia dipingono un quadro molto più negativo di quello reale.

Day 13
VERB CONSTRUCTIONS

1 ho

2 è

3 è

4 ha

5 Hanno

6 è

7 è

8 Abbiamo

9 sono

10–11 è; abbiamo

12 Ogni mattina aspettiamo l'autobus alla stessa fermata.

13 Ho cercato quei documenti ma non li ho trovati.

14 Che cosa hai risposto a Maurizio?

15 Guardavano le nostre fotografie.

16 Non abbiamo ancora telefonato a Federica.

17 Laura non permette ai suoi bambini di andare a dormire tardi.

18 Sai giocare a scacchi?

19 Ci siamo congratulati con Pietro per la sua laurea.

20 Perché ridi di questa situazione?

21 Ancora una volta hai disobbedito ai tuoi genitori.

22 Purtroppo questa decisione non dipende da me.

23 Avrà ricevuto una brutta notizia.

24 Sarà giù.

25 Avrà litigato di nuovo con il suo ragazzo.

26 Avrà mal di denti.

27 Vorrà fare qualcos'altro.

28 Avrà avuto un'offerta migliore.

29 Avrà deciso di andare all'università.

30 Non sarà sicuro di saper fare il lavoro.

Day 14
USING THE SUBJUNCTIVE

1 Speriamo che non sia troppo tardi.

2 Credi/credete davvero che lei abbia ragione?

3 Non è detto che il nostro problema maggiore sia la mancanza di fondi.

4 Non vedo l'ora che comincino le vacanze!

5 Temo che la tua spiegazione sia poco convincente.

6 Penso che abbiano preso la decisione più sensata.

7 Può darsi che ci siano due possibilità di interpretazione.

8 Mettiamo che lei abbia già scoperto la verità.

9 Può darsi che la lettera non sia arrivata.

10 Non è detto che tutti siano d'accordo con te.

11 È una vergogna che gli anziani siano trattati in questo modo.

12 È giusto che i dipendenti facciano sciopero.

13 Era una fortuna che la piscina fosse aperta.

14 È normale che i giovani vogliano trasmissioni divertenti.

15 Era prevedibile che gli uomini politici dessero risposte evasive.

16 Bisogna che vi sbrighiate se volete uscire.

17 Bisognava che vi sbrigaste se volevate uscire.

18 È essenziale che tu finisca prima di domani.

19 È importante che ogni opinione venga ascoltata.

20 È ora che decidiate che cosa volete fare.

21 È un'assurdità/È assurdo che quest'ufficio sia sempre chiuso.

22 È incredibile che abbia vinto tutti quei soldi.

23 Per assurda che ti possa sembrare, la mia decisione è definitiva.

24 Se solo me ne fossi accorto/a in tempo, avrei agito diversamente.

25 Gli parlava come se fosse il loro padre.

26 Che io sappia, non legge romanzi gialli.

27 È un grande scrittore e, sia detto per inciso, lo è anche sua moglie.

28 Vada come vada, io sono dalla tua parte.

29 Per bello che sia, è talmente egocentrico che non piace a nessuno.

30 Tratta la mia casa come se fosse la sua.

Day 15
PASSIVE SENTENCES

1 Una donna guidava la macchina

2 ha provocato

3 siano causati

4 saranno rifiutati da tutti

5 non è stata ancora riparata dall'idraulico

6 era già stata fatta dai ragazzi

7 fosse guidata da una donna

8 l'auto sarebbe stata guidata da una donna

9 Assicuratevi che le scarpe sporche di fango non vengano lasciate sul pavimento.

10 Molto spesso i pasti vengono consumati davanti alla televisione.

11 Le auto venivano sempre parcheggiate in doppia fila.

12 La spiegazione verrà ripetuta domani.

13 Questi moduli vanno compilati e consegnati entro domani.

14 Il tuo vestito andrebbe accorciato un po'.

15 La mia macchina andrà revisionata ad aprile.

16 Pensavo che queste lettere non andassero spedite oggi.

17 Credo che questa decisione vada presa da tutti.

18 Le piante da appartamento non vanno innaffiate troppo.

19 Nella confusione, la mia bella sciarpa è andata persa.

20 Mettiamo qui le chiavi, in modo che non vadano dimenticate.

21 Ancora una volta i nostri sforzi sono andati sprecati.

22 I due sciatori sono rimasti sepolti da una valanga.

23 Rimarrete scioccati anche voi quando saprete quello che è successo.

24 Invece di alzarsi in piedi, gli spettatori erano rimasti seduti.

25 Mi hanno fatto vedere il nuovo appartamento.

26 Ci avevano chiesto di pagare per le fotocopie.

27 Le hanno detto di non uscire.

28 Gli fanno troppi regali./Fanno loro troppi regali.

29 Gli promisero/hanno promesso una promozione.

30 Ti/Vi stavano vendendo una macchina difettosa!

Day 16
RHETORICAL SIGNPOSTS AND LOGICAL CONNECTORS

1 prima di tutto

2 In primo luogo

3 Tutto sommato/In definitiva

4 In secondo luogo

5 in linea di massima

6 In fin dei conti

7 sostanzialmente/in sostanza

8 Questo problema tocca da vicino sia i giovani che gli anziani/non solo i giovani, ma anche gli anziani/i giovani come pure gli anziani/tanto i giovani quanto gli anziani.

9 I dipendenti di questa ditta sono sfruttati e allo stesso tempo sottopagati./ Oltre ad essere sfruttati, i dipendenti di questa ditta sono sottopagati.

10 La piscina è aperta sia d'estate che d'inverno.

11 I giovani telespettatori vorrebbero trasmissioni istruttive e allo stesso tempo divertenti/istruttive oltre che divertenti/non solo istruttive ma anche divertenti.

12 Gli uomini politici, sia di destra che di sinistra/non solo di destra, ma anche di sinistra hanno dato risposte evasive.

13 tanto che/al punto che

14 ecco perché

15 di conseguenza

16 perciò/quindi/per cui/pertanto

17 dunque/per cui/pertanto

18 in modo da

19 Dato che ti sei scusato, non hai nulla da temere.

20 Visto che sono già le sei, propongo che ci fermiamo qui.

21 L'obesità è in aumento in quanto le abitudini alimentari degli adolescenti sono fondamentalmente sbagliate.

22 Hanno fatto male a disfarsi della loro auto vecchia, considerato che non sono sicuri di quando arriverà quella nuova.

23 Siccome/Dal momento che lo avevano aiutato, l'autore ha ringraziato tutti i suoi collaboratori.

24 Mi aveva detto che l'avrei trovata in ufficio, eppure non c'era.

25 L'economia è in continua crescita anche se i prezzi continuano a salire.

26 Non è un tentativo di mediazione, bensì/piuttosto una vera provocazione.

27 Non abbiamo molto tempo, quindi/ perciò/pertanto/ di conseguenza faremmo meglio a sbrigarci.

28 A Lorenzo non piaceva l'estate dato che/per il fatto che/siccome soffriva di raffreddore da fieno.

29 Shakespeare è considerato un

autore
fondamentale, ecco
perché/perciò lo
leggete a scuola.

30 Dovranno pagare
in contanti
siccome/dal
momento che/dato
che non porteranno
la carta di credito.

Day 17
INFINITIVE VS.
GERUND

1 allenarti
2 parlare
3 pensare
4 andare
5 fare
6 urlare/gridare
7 viaggiare
8 ballare
9 aver finito
10 esser caduta
11 aver parlato
12 esser stati
13 Nuotare
14 giocare
15 uscire
16 mentre
passeggiavo
17 che aspettavano
18 Quando compri
19 Sentendomi
20 Avendo ricevuto
21 sperando
22 Pur conoscendolo
23 Pur vivendo/
abitando
24 sorridente
25 sorprendente
26 Pur avendo fatto
27 Facendo
28 Fare

29 fare/che faceva
30 aver fatto

Day 18
POLITICS AND
CURRENT AFFAIRS

1 the House of
Commons
2 la Camera dei Lord
3 the extreme right-
wing parties
4 i partiti di sinistra
5 i partiti di centro
6 the silent majority
7 ethnic minorities
8 i partiti di
minoranza
9 la maggioranza
degli italiani
10 peace talks
11 il trattato di pace
12 A che ora è stato
raggiunto l'accordo
sul bilancio
dell'Unione Europea?
13 Per chi voterai alle
elezioni politiche?
14–15 È difficile per il
primo ministro di un
governo di
minoranza imporre il
programma
legislativo che ha
promesso
all'elettorato.
16 people power
17 petty bourgeois
aspirations
18 burocratico
19 un dittatore
20 dittatoriale
21 l'anarchia
22 il movimento per i
diritti civili

23 la carta d'identità
24–25 British
conservatism has
very little in
common with the
political right in the
United States.
26–28 Ultimately he's
a follower of the
right-wing
tendencies of his
party, despite his
past as a
representative of the
centre-left.
29–30 The trade
unions have lost a
great deal of the
power they enjoyed
in the Seventies.

Day 19
USING IMPERATIVES
AND PRONOUNS
CORRECTLY

1 Comprateglielo!
2 Glieli compri!
3 Compracelo!
4 Vendimene una!
5 Non
vendiamoglielo!
6 Finiscine uno!
7 Apritegli la porta!
8 Non apriamone
nessuno!
9 Bevilo!
10 Beviamocene una
insieme!
11 Non bevetene
troppo!
12 Sceglieteglielo voi!
13 Ne scelga uno!
14 Non togliermelo
di mano!

15 Lo tenga stretto!

16 Tienimelo un momento!

17 Stallo a sentire!

18 Non ne abbia paura!

19 Non esserne gelosa!

20 Dimmi la verità!

21 Diglielo!

22 Ditecelo!

23 Vacci!

24 Fammi un favore!

25 Faccelo!

26 Daccela!

27 Datecene uno!

28 Gliele dia!

29 Me lo faccia sapere!

30 Non glielo dica!

Day 20
SCIENCE AND THE ENVIRONMENT

1 metafisico/-a

2 la fisica nucleare

3 un/una chimico/-a

4 genetic engineering

5 l'astrologia, astrologico, l'astrologo/-a

6 l'antropologia, antropologico, l'antropologo/-a

7 la psicologia, psicologico, lo/la psicologo/-a

8 test-tube babies

9 at the experimental stage

10 un'indagine

11 Anche se non era un genio, era coscienziosa e prendeva sempre voti discreti.

12 Ma come puoi credere all'astrologia?

13 I progetti di ricerca scientifica sono a volte molto costosi ed è perciò abbastanza difficile ottenere i finanziamenti necessari.

14–15 I progressi della genetica fanno paura ad alcuni, che li paragonano agli esperimenti del dottor Frankenstein.

16 environmental decline

17 fake fur

18 l'impatto ambientale

19 the greenhouse effect

20 the rain forest

21 la pioggia acida

22 industrial waste

23 toxic waste

24 biodegradabile

25 i pesticidi

26 environmental balance

27 climate changes

28 prodotti modificati geneticamente

29 Mi preoccupano le questioni ambientali, particolarmente quello che dicono gli scienziati sull'effetto-serra.

30 L'inquinamento del Mediterraneo, specialmente quello causato da chiazze di petrolio e da scarichi chimici e industriali, è una vera tragedia.

Day 21
IMPERSONAL AND PASSIVE CONSTRUCTIONS WITH SI

1 parlerà

2 vedono

3 firmeranno

4 riceveva

5 fanno

6 fa

7 si deve fare

8 ci si annoia

9 si poteva comprare

10 si dovrebbe mangiare

11 ci si vuole riposare

12 ci si sposerà

13 Quando ci si sente depressi, si deve fare uno sforzo per condurre una vita normale.

14 Non credi anche tu che d'inverno ci si senta più stanchi?

15 Si dovrebbe essere disposti ad accettare il punto di vista altrui anche se non si è contenti della situazione.

16 Pensavo che ci si sentisse tutti più buoni a Natale!

17 Ci si ritiene fortunati di essere nati in questo secolo?

18 La chirurgia plastica è la soluzione estrema se si è insoddisfatte del proprio aspetto.

19 Le spese non si sono mai pagate in contanti.

20 Quando si sarebbe tenuta questa riunione?

21 In questo libro non si è capito niente.

22 Per perdere peso si sarebbe dovuta fare più ginnastica.

23 Purtroppo non si è avuto il tempo di discutere la faccenda.

24 Se si vuole diventare giornalisti, si deve andare facilmente d'accordo con la gente.

25 È importante che si sappiano memorizzare e riprodurre bene molte informazioni.

26 È indispensabile che si sia disposti a lavorare per molte ore, anche di notte.

27 Si potrà fare carriera se si sarà veloci, accurati e originali quando si scriveranno gli articoli.

28 Quando si sarà lavorato per un giornale o una stazione televisiva

per parecchi anni, si avrà la possibilità di viaggiare e di vivere all'estero.

29 Si conosceranno persone importanti e persone qualunque.

30 Si sarà strumenti di diffusione dell'informazione e di comunicazione.

Day 22
EDUCATION

1 la scuola statale
2 l'insegnamento
3 il/la compagno/a di appartamento
4 la lezione privata
5 il materiale
6 le facoltà mentali
7 universale
8 studioso
9–10 In quanti eravate in classe alla scuola elementare?
11–12 La vita studentesca non è fatta solo di studio.

13–15 Nelle facoltà universitarie, gli esami sono corretti dallo stesso docente che ha tenuto le lezioni.

16–18 Negli istituti tecnici statali non si deve portare la divisa, ma nei licei privati e in alcuni collegi sì.

19–21 Tutti i mercoledì Luca taglia la scuola con un compagno di classe per evitare la lezione di chimica.

22–24 Quando andava a scuola mio padre, l'informatica non esisteva. Doveva studiare filosofia, ma non andava molto bene a scuola.

25 la correzione
26 corretto
27 istruttivo

28–30

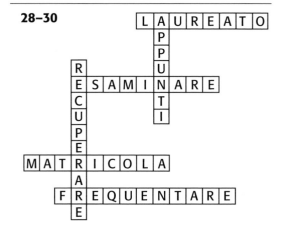

Day 23
CONDITIONAL
SENTENCES
1 C
2 Q
3 C
4 Q
5 C
6 Q
7 C
8 a
9 c
10 X
11 X
12 b
13 avessi detto
14 si arrabbieranno
15 fossi
16 potessimo
17 andrebbero
18 si comprerebbe
19 vedi
20 avrei invitata
21 ha perso
22 mancasse
23 è mancato
24 Senza un indirizzo fisso/non avendo un indirizzo fisso
25 Con un po' di fortuna/Avendo avuto un po' di fortuna
26 In caso di incendio
27 Se avessi i soldi, andrei in vacanza.
28 Se tu fossi/sarai più ottimista, la vita ti sembrerebbe/sembrerà più bella.
29 Se non fossero stufi della matematica,
avrebbero finito di studiare.
30 Se non fumasse tantissimo, non tossirebbe di continuo.

Day 24
DIALOGUE AND
REPORTED SPEECH
1 ritiene
2 abbiamo fatto notare
3 hanno ammesso
4 ha annunciato/annunciò
5 aveva aggiunto
6 spiegò/ha spiegato
7 Notò/Ha notato
8 strillò
9 balbettai
10 ruggì
11 ribatté
12 gemette
13 con voce risentita
14 tremando
15 con aria desolata
16 con voce appassionata
17 con voce/aria sarcastica
18 Marisa sarebbe stata felicissima di sentirci. Paul had assured us that Marisa would be really pleased to hear from us.
19 sarebbe già partita. They objected that she would have left already.
20 era dimagrito molto. They observed that he
had lost a lot of weight.
21 il tasso di disoccupazione avrebbe dovuto abbassarsi/si sarebbe dovuto abbassare notevolmente. The government stated that the unemployment rate should fall considerably.
22 non mi sopportava più. She had shouted that she could not stand me anymore.
23 non avrebbe avuto tempo di leggere l'articolo. He had clarified that he would not have time to read the article.
24 Secondo la segretaria, sarebbe malato da tre giorni.
25 Secondo la leggenda, Roma sarebbe stata fondata da due gemelli, Romolo e Remo.
26 Secondo fonti autorevoli, i capi di stato si sarebbero incontrati segretamente per discutere la crisi.
27 Secondo le autorità sportive, molti atleti farebbero

regolarmente uso di sostanze anabolizzanti.

28 Secondo i testimoni, l'imputato avrebbe rubato quadri e gioielli al fratello.

29 – Non partirò fino a lunedì – aveva ammesso Sofia.

30 – Potete darmi una mano? – ci domandò la nostra vicina.

Day 25
MODAL VERBS

1 Potrei lasciare un messaggio?

2 Non è potuto/riuscito ad arrivare in tempo.

3 A tre anni sapeva già leggere.

4 Possiamo vederci giovedì prossimo, se per te va bene.

5 Potremmo vederci giovedì prossimo, se per te andasse bene.

6 Perché non posso uscire?

7 Sono troppo giovani, non sono in grado di capire certe scelte.

8 Ho le dita troppo grosse, non riesco ad infilare l'ago.

9 Potete fare come volete.

10 Qualsiasi cosa accada, te lo farò sapere.

11 Questo potrebbe essere difficile.

12 Hanno legato il cane per paura che scappasse.

13 Avresti potuto dirmelo prima!

14 Spero che riesca a trovare il lavoro che cerca.

15 Daniele non risponde: può darsi che sia già uscito/sarà già uscito/forse è già uscito.

16 Che cosa dovrei fare?

17 Se telefonano, digli che li richiamerò più tardi.

18 Non so se dovrei parlarne con Giacomo.

19 A quanti anni si dovrebbe andare in pensione, secondo te?

20 Se vincessi al lotto, andrei subito in pensione!

21 Come vedi, ho dovuto farlo.

22 Andrei in Italia se potessi.

23 Patrizia non vuole saperne di mettere in ordine la sua camera.

24 La vecchietta passava ore ed ore affacciata alla finestra.

25 I bambini staranno con noi stasera.

26 Non voleva far nulla per aiutarli.

27 Mi daresti una mano?

28 Al posto tuo, non avrei risposto così.

29 A quest'ora, avrà finito di parlare col medico.

30 Non volete sedervi cinque minuti?

Day 26
HEALTH

1 'flu symptoms

2 una reazione allergica

3 il Servizio Sanitario Nazionale

4 la sieropositività

5 esaurito/a

6 cosmetic surgery

7 to undergo a difficult operation

8 la vaccinazione

9 l'anestetista

10 anestetizzare

11 Perché non hai salutato Carlo? – Non l'avevo visto.

12 Molti coloranti alimentari sono stati proibiti perché hanno proprietà cancerogene.

13 Siete stati vaccinati contro la tubercolosi?

14 L'ambulatorio del Dottor Ferraris è aperto per le visite ai pazienti dalle 2 alle 4.

15–16 Hai anche tu il raffreddore da fieno? – No, ma sono allergico/-a ai peli dei gatti.

17 Quando l'ho visto estrarre la pistola, ho sudato freddo dalla paura.

18–19 Si sente bene Laura? Ha l'aria strana. – Non so, forse ha un po' d'influenza.

20 pneumonia
21 la bronchite
22 l'artrite
23 l'otite
24 la tonsillite
25 l'appendicite
26–30 i brividi – shivers
  la febbre – temperature, fever
  l'infarto – heart attack
  la ricetta – prescription
  la salute – health
  lo sfogo – rash
  sieropositivo – HIV positive
  stressante – stressful
  lo svenimento – fainting fit
  la varicella – chicken pox

Day 27
USING POSSESSIVES CORRECTLY

1 Hai visto il suo appartamento nuovo?
2 Ti piacciono i suoi amici?
3 Ti piacciono le sue amiche?
4 I loro bambini sono molto vivaci.
5 La sua popolazione è diminuita.
6 Le loro piante sono davvero rigogliose.
7 Il loro appartamento è in vendita.
8–10 Ernesto, ti presento mio fratello Giorgio, la mia sorellina Gigliola e i miei nonni materni.

11–12 Questa è la mia seconda moglie Paola e queste sono le nostre figlie gemelle, Anna e Cristina.

13–14 Vorrei presentarti il mio figlio più grande, Davide, e la sua fidanzata, Alessandra.

15 Quasi tutte le specie animali proteggono i loro piccoli.

16–18 Non preoccuparti, questo ritardo non è colpa tua. Appena arriviamo a casa mia, telefoniamo ai tuoi.

19 Marina è una mia amica.

20 Alberto è un suo collega.

21 Viene alla festa con quattro (delle) sue cugine.
22 Abbiamo cenato con alcuni/dei nostri clienti (con qualche nostro cliente).
23 Non capisco questo tuo/vostro atteggiamento.
24 Quei tuoi/vostri amici proprio non mi piacciono.
25 Ho riletto tutte le sue lettere.
26–27 Mi si è guastato il computer, ma per fortuna posso usare quello di mio fratello.
28 Susanna ha perso la carta d'identità.
29–30 Se vado ad abitare da solo, chi mi laverà i vestiti e chi mi farà la spesa?

Day 28
FALSE FRIENDS
1 colta
2 una discussione molto accesa
3–4 biblioteca, restituire
5 attrezzature
6 educati
7 personaggi
8 Supponevo
9 genitori
10 efficaci
11 guarita
12 comprensivo
13 finalmente

14 sensato
15 annoiata
16 Istruzione
17 mi ero reso/a conto
18 è finanziata/sostenuta
19 simpatico
20–21 efficaci, coerente
22 alternativa
23 plastica
24 marginale
25 necessità
26 elettricità
27–28 glorioso, avventuroso
29 espressione
30 inflessibile

Day 29
REVISION: KEY POINTS
1–2 Questo programma di studi è radicale e progressista e offre ottime opportunità di sviluppo.
3 Preferirei parlare con chi mi ha scritto la lettera che ho ricevuto ieri.
4 Per favore, ricordatevi di restituire tutto ciò/quello che vi è stato prestato dalla scuola.
5 Questo articolo non è troppo difficile da capire e sono sicuro che mi servirà molto.
6 Il medico viene tutti i pomeriggi, ma il

paziente sta decisamente meglio.
7 Il congresso avrà luogo fra due mesi e si terrà ancora una volta nella nostra Sede di Milano.
8 Da un momento all'altro comincerà lo spettacolo.
9 Ti interessa l'arte moderna? – Mi incuriosisce, ma spesso le opere non mi piacciono molto.
10 Vi sono bastati i soldi che vi ho dato? – Sì, grazie, e il film ci è piaciuto molto.
11 Mentre facevamo la spesa, abbiamo incontrato il mio insegnante di matematica.
12 Quando venivano a trovarci, eravamo sempre felici di vederli.
13 Giulia ha cominciato a studiare il francese quando aveva sette anni.
14 Chi ha rotto questo bicchiere? – Sarà stato/Forse è stato/Può darsi che sia stato Franco, prima lavava/stava lavando i piatti.
15 È deludente che i giovani leggano così pochi libri.

16 Era ora che arrivaste! Vi aspettiamo da mezz'ora!

17 A sentire come era stata condotta la selezione, sono rimasta veramente amareggiata.

18 Mi hanno mandato un modulo che va assolutamente compilato entro domani.

19 Dopo aver scritto una lettera ai suoi genitori, è partito.

20 Si arrabbiano sempre parlando di politica, ma preferiscono discutere apertamente le cose.

21 Per favore, signora, mi porti delle carote.

22 Non farmi stare in pensiero, Roberto, torna presto.

23 Entro quando si deve finire questa relazione?

24 Quando si è viziati come lui, si pretende sempre molto.

25 Se me lo avessi chiesto, ti avrei aiutata.

26 Se piove/Se piovesse, andremo al cinema invece che al parco.

27 Non immaginavo che sapessi sciare così bene.

28 Se te lo chiede/chiedesse, dagli il mio indirizzo.

29 Mio fratello non ha fatto l'università, ma la mia sorella minore ha studiato medicina.

30 Sei un impiccione, fatti gli affari tuoi!

Day 30
VOCABULARY
REVISION TEST

1 sfacciato/-a, un/-a ficcanaso

2 la puntata, un film dell'orrore

3 lo stadio, suonare uno strumento

4 il capitolo, la narrativa

5 recitare, il quadro

6 la libertà, perdere

7 settentrionale, la percentuale

8 disimpegnato/-a, anticonformista

9 egoista, immaturo/-a

10 indifferente, disinvolto/-a

11 inoltre, per lo più

12 i politici, il potere

13 la borghesia, i diritti civili

14 un colpo di genio, ingegnoso

15 riciclare, l'inquinamento

16 la materia, essere laureato/-a in

17 precisare, sussurrare

18 per sbaglio, a poco a poco

19 stressante, guarire

20 colto/-a, finalmente

21 visto che, dal momento che

22 del resto, tuttavia

23 di conseguenza, pertanto

24 Vuoi sempre fare di testa tua: sei davvero testardo/-a!

25 Non a tutti piace lo stile liberty, è una questione di gusti personali.

26 Quasi tutti i quotidiani italiani contengono ormai uno o più inserti.

27 Segue ora un servizio dal nostro inviato in Libano.

28 Cerca di leggere *Seta*, è un romanzo davvero fuori del comune.

29 Se gli agricoltori non ricevessero le sovvenzioni statali, molti fallirebbero.

30 Negli ultimi anni sono stati fatti grandi progressi nella lotta contro il cancro.

Bibliography

Reference grammars
Denise De Rôme, *Soluzioni! A Practical Guide to Italian Grammar*
    (Arnold, 2003)
M. Maiden and C. Robustelli, *A Reference Grammar of Modern Italian*
    (Arnold, 2000)
A. Proudfoot and F. Cardo, *Modern Italian Grammar* (Routledge, 1997)

Exercises
A. Bianchi and C. Boscolo, *Practising Italian Grammar* (Arnold, 2003)
A. Proudfoot and F. Cardo, *Modern Italian Grammar Workbook* (Routledge,
    1999)

Index